BATH IN THE AGE OF REFORM

(1830–1841) by John Wroughton

In the early part of the nineteenth century Bath still wore something of the air of gentility it had inherited from the days when the city was the centre of fashion. It still enjoyed the patronage of wealth, albeit from a nouveau riche middle-class. Its attitude toward the working classes was almost paternal. There are no harrowing stories of extreme poverty, or of the cruel exploitation of children. Because there was no industry in Bath then, the rate of change that was being accelerated elsewhere by the Industrial Revolution was slower.

Yet, surprisingly, the citizens of Bath, who might have been expected to have been reluctant to accept change, gave a considerable lead to reform. There were very lively scenes in the city during the parliamentary election of 1832. These are fully described in this detailed study of Bath and its people at a time when the old order was giving way to a new.

BATH
IN THE AGE OF REFORM

(1830-1841)

Edited by

JOHN WROUGHTON

MORGAN BOOKS

37 Broad Street, Bath, Somerset, England

First published 1972

© John Wroughton

SBN   903044   05   6

Made and Printed in Great Britain by

COWARD & GERRISH LTD., LARKHALL, BATH, SOMERSET

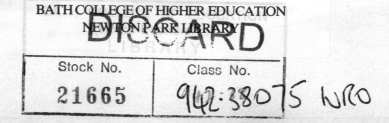

Edited by

JOHN WROUGHTON, M.A. (Oxon.)
Senior History Master, King Edward's School, Bath

Foreword by

B. H. HOLBECHE, M.A. (Cantab.), J.P.
Headmaster, King Edward's School, Bath

Contributors

STEPHEN BROOKS, B.A. (Oxon.)
Scholar of Hertford College, Oxford

DAVID DETHRIDGE
Scholar of The Queen's College, Oxford

MARTIN HEMMINGS
Commoner of Exeter College, Oxford

MARK ROBERTS
Commoner of Hertford College, Oxford

RICHARD SALTER
Scholar of Exeter College, Oxford

BRIAN WEIGHT
Exhibitioner of Trinity College, Cambridge

STEPHEN WILLIAMS
Scholar of Trinity College, Cambridge

Foreword

IT gives me great pleasure, as Headmaster of King Edward's School and as President of the Headmasters' Association for 1970, to commend this volume of explorations into *Bath in the Age of Reform* to the general public. There is a wealth of literature on the glories of this Georgian City in the eighteenth century, but nineteenth century Bath has been curiously neglected. These essays represent an attempt to remedy this deficiency by presenting the fruits of original research into a period which, for Bath at least, was unique in the history of the Industrial Revolution.

Again, this collection of related essays amply demonstrates what admirable use really able Sixth Formers can make of primary sources; for printed material on Bath during this period is almost non-existent, so that the contributors had to forage for all their evidence in the City Records Office and Reference Library. In the first place they did so as part of their preparation for Oxford or Cambridge Scholarships or as individual projects for their Advanced Level examinations. The very favourable comments made by their assessors encouraged us to consider the possibility of a joint publication since the projects were all concerned by chance with the period from 1830–1841. With this in mind, each writer has revised and enlarged his contribution; while the chapters on 'Bath and its Workers' and 'Bath and its Entertainments' have been added to fill two significant gaps in the initial range of topics.

Unquestionably the inspiration for this publication came from my Senior History Master, Mr. John Wroughton, who is himself the author of several texts on the Civil War. As editor of this publication, he would be the first to join me in paying tribute to the liveliness and dedication of his own pupils whose research was spread over the years 1967 to 1969. They richly deserve separate mention in this Foreword:

Stephen Brooks, Scholar of Hertford College, Oxford;
David Dethridge, Scholar of The Queen's College, Oxford;
Martin Hemmings, Exeter College, Oxford;
Mark Roberts, Hertford College, Oxford;
Richard Salter, Scholar of Exeter College, Oxford;
Brian Weight, Exhibitioner of Trinity College, Cambridge;
Stephen Williams, Scholar of Trinity College, Cambridge.

Finally, we hope that their efforts, guided by Mr. Wroughton, will not only inspire other young historians to similar achievements but also will prove to be of interest to the public at large.

BRIAN H. HOLBECHE

Acknowledgements

THE Editor wishes to express his sincere thanks to the following people who have helped considerably in the production of this book:

The Governors and Headmaster of King Edward's School, Bath, for their encouragement;

Martin Cryer, Peter Lane, Robert Wall and Michael Gibbons, his Sixth Form pupils, for their research on the 1841 Census Returns in the Public Records Office, London;

Mr. E. H. Bungay, his colleague, for his assistance with the illustrations;

Mr. N. J. L. Pearce, the Town Clerk, and Mr. Peter Pagan, the City Librarian, for permission to reproduce archive material and illustrations;

Mr. R. Bryant, the City Archivist, and the staff of the Bath Reference Library for their patience and advice;

Dr. R. A. Buchanan for his interest;

Mrs. Helen Panter for topographical information;

Mrs. T. F. Rabbitts for her accurate and cheerful typing of the manuscript.

Finally, he would like to thank his team of young and talented contributors (all former pupils) for their enthusiasm, drive and application. It has been a real privilege and pleasure to work with them at the start of their promising academic careers.

J.P.W.

Contents

Illustrations

Introduction

THE AGE OF REFORM

JOHN WROUGHTON

REVOLUTION in industry, wars against France and a national conscience aroused by Wesley and the Evangelicals had together created the need for an Age of Reform. Disease-ridden slums, long working hours, cramped factories, low wages, unemployment, corrupt local governments, rotten boroughs all cried out for reform. The cry resounded through England in the marching feet of the Blanketeers, the fearless denunciations of Cobbett in his *Twopenny Trash* and the impassioned pleas of 'Orator' Henry Hunt at mass meetings in Manchester. Lord Liverpool and his Tories, fearing that the Bastille would also fall in England, shut their ears and loaded their rifles. The Peterloo Massacre (1819) and the Six Acts (1819) put the rabble firmly in its place.

But reform could only be delayed, not averted. By 1830 Lord Grey and his Whigs had realised that Bastilles could best be saved after all by a few well-chosen reforms. The reforms they chose were not to everyone's liking. Indeed it is doubtful whether Grey and Melbourne would have rated highly in any popularity poll of the day.

It is certainly questionable whether these years should be called the Age of Reform at all. What in fact happened? The vote was given to an extra few thousand of the middle class, workhouses were set up to discourage people from becoming poor, slavery was abolished in the empire but not in factories, local governments were changed to stimulate efficiency—and police forces were established to deal with protests against the other 'reforms'. Little was actually *done* to grapple with the terrible effects on human beings of the Industrial Revolution, which was then at its peak. Royal Commissions, it is true, abounded on this, that and the other. But their

1

reports on unemployment, conditions in factories and mines, public health and child labour were confined to dusty shelves till later.

This, nevertheless, was a period of important change which helped to lay the foundations of Victorian England. How did Bath react to these decisions at Westminster? We hope in the following pages to discover what part she played in the Age of Reform. It was, as we shall see, both considerable and unexpected.

In 1831 Bath was a town of impressive size. Its population of 50,802, which was one of the largest in the west, was expanding.[1] Apparently vigorous in its growth, Bath at first sight seemed typical of all large cities in the Industrial Revolution. And yet it was not. It *had* no industry. Indeed, the Industrial Revolution had passed it by virtually unscathed. Ironically this was more a cause for regret than for rejoicing. To be *sure* of a place in Victorian England, Bath needed the sort of upheaval that Manchester and Birmingham were to suffer. Looking back, of course, we can be thankful that it managed without. But Bath almost perished in the cause of elegance.

In the eighteenth century the City had been both aristocratic and prosperous, a health resort of the rich. The buildings which had housed them still remained; the people who had served them still remained—but Beau Nash had gone and the upper classes now preferred Brighton. Bath lost its social vigour; it became middle-aged and middle-class (see Chapter Five). Men of lower birth and newly-acquired wealth moved in to fill the vacuum. They lacked the panâche of their predecessors; they plunged the City into medio-crity. But for the time being they kept it alive. Their patronage during the Age of Reform ensured economic stability for the City and employment for its workers. So Bath hung on as an anachronism till the Bristol commuter, the tourist on the cheap-day excursion, the Admiralty and the University brought meaning back to its existence.

Yet in spite of its social decline, Bath in a surprising way retained its reputation for leadership. A new rôle had emerged. The City became, not a cultural centre, but a centre of radical thought and administrative experiment. 'A place which has the reproach of being *a hot-bed for revolution*', complained a Tory poster in 1837. Quiet, respectable Bath not only returned two radical M.P.s after the Great

---

[1]This figure represents the Parliamentary boundary of the city and includes the parishes of St. James, St. Michael's, St. Peter and St. Paul, Walcot, Bathwick, Lyncombe and Widcombe. The *old* city consisted of the first four parishes which housed 38,003 people.

Reform Bill in 1832 (see Chapter Two), but also became a meeting place for Chartists from 1837 (see Chapter One).

> Here we have the Whig Mayor of Bath granting the use of the Guildhall to persons who have made it the arena of discussion strikingly resembling, in almost everything but talent, those which took place in the Hall of the Jacobins, so memorable during the time of the first French Revolution . . . Here we have the Sheriff of Bath, with a Russellite magistrate and sundry Town Councillors, applauding second-hand French slang about 'fraternisation', about 'frightening' the aristocracy into the granting of 'the people's rights' . . .[2]

Radical thought in Bath was clearly not the monopoly of the discontented crowd. Local political leaders, to a greater or lesser extent, shared this progressive outlook. Bath's old Corporation believed not only in parliamentary reform in 1832, but also in some measure of reform for itself in 1835 (see Chapter Seven). The City was amongst the first to set up the new Poor Law system (see Chapter Three), as well as the new Police Force in 1836 (see Chapter Eight). Although slums existed, its attitude to public health was enlightened for the times (see Chapter Four). One of the pioneers of Turnpike Trusts in 1707, Bath was quick to share in the benefits of the new Great Western Railway (see Chapter Six).

Bath in 1841 was progressive, compassionate and paternalistic. Its elegance remained; its stability survived. It was a city of memories —a city of the retired and the genteel. It was also a city of hopes— a city of the Chartist and the Radical. It was a city vigorous and alive in thought; a city courageous in experiment. But it was also a city lost in its dreams; a city still mesmerised by the swirling skirts of the Grand Balls; a city enslaved by its history and its run-down entertainments industry. Yet there was, nevertheless, something essentially good about Bath in the Age of Reform. It treated people decently.

[2]*Bath Chronicle*, 23rd December, 1841.

CHAPTER ONE

Bath and its Workers

JOHN WROUGHTON

THE visitant is well aware that Bath is not a city of trade. No manufactures worthy of notice is carried on within its limits, nor is it the resort of commerce . . . Of all places in the Kingdom, Bath is best fitted for the retirement of individuals with independent incomes, whether small or large. For those past the meridian of life, its quietness, beautiful neighbourhood, and warmth of climate, particularly recommend it . . . Trade in Bath consists principally in the sale of articles connected with the refinements, rather than the necessities of life.

In these words *The Bath Visitant* of 1839 describes the unique features of local City life. From the eighteenth century Bath, a health and holiday resort, had attracted a wealthy consumer society within its walls. Its workers, therefore, served not the mass-production needs of newly-mechanised industries, but the quality market of services and hand-made luxury goods. An analysis of the Census returns shows that this was still largely the case even as late as 1841.

Out of a total *working* population of 16,613[1] people in the main City parishes of St. James, St. Peter & St. Paul, St. Michael's, and Walcot, 33·7 per cent. were engaged in domestic service—a clear indication that Bath abounded in professional classes, affluent visitors and those of 'independent means'. A large number of male and female servants (5,108 in all) combined with housekeepers, gardeners, charwomen, grooms, cooks, stewards and footmen to make up this army of personal attendants. By far the greatest proportion of these lived or lodged in Walcot.

[1]The *total* population of these four parishes in 1841 was 38,304.

Another 11·5 per cent. served the clothing needs of a fashion-conscious society. 695 people were involved in dressmaking, 491 in tailoring, 241 in millinery and 105 in bonnet making. Needlewomen, seamstresses, hatters, hosiers and staymakers completed the number of those who helped to maintain Bath's tradition of sartorial elegance. The elegance of their homes was taken care of by the skill of a further 11 per cent. who were involved in small crafts of varying kinds. Cabinetmakers, pipemakers, clockmakers, chairmakers, bellowsmakers, silversmiths, goldsmiths, locksmiths, wheelchair-makers, saddlers, shoemakers, cordwainers, printers, engravers, gunmakers, basketmakers, umbrellamakers all found a ready market in the comfortable streets of Bath.

To complete the ever-ready range of services which awaited the visitor, 9 per cent. of the working population were employed as shopkeepers, traders and distributors of goods (from milkmen to hawkers); 7·7 per cent. were involved in building and constructional work (carpenters, masons, plasterers, plumbers, painters, quarrymen, etc.); 5·9 per cent. offered professional services (surgeons, nurses, teachers, solicitors, stockbrokers, accountants, bankers, clergy, dentists, auctioneers, surveyors, opticians, etc.); 4 per cent. provided entertainment and hospitality to those who could afford it (inn-keepers, publicans, musicians, comedians, dancers, chairmen, newspaper reporters, writers, coachmen, ostlers, etc.); 3·9 per cent. gave services of a more menial kind (washerwomen, sweeps, messengers, etc.); and 0·7 per cent. were City officials who helped to see that the amenities worked smoothly and were not abused (policemen, toll collectors, watermen, tax collectors, postmen, town cryers, librarian, coroner, excise officials, lamplighters, baths superintendent, river inspectors, mayor's officers, etc.)

All-in-all, as many as 87·4 per cent. of all those who worked in the main City parishes devoted their time and energy to providing services and luxuries for the large number of wealthy consumers. Only 1·4 per cent. were engaged as trained workers in what can be called major industry (though others clearly lived in the outlying parishes of Lyncombe and Widcombe). Of these most were employed in the woollen cloth industry at Twerton (see later); in small iron or brass foundries; in tin works; in road or railway construction; at the gas works; in the pin factory; or in one of the local breweries. According to *The New Bath Guide* in 1834 there were three or four 'very capital breweries in the city, where an extensive foreign and home trade is carried on in porter, pale-beer and ale'. There were also several smaller ones 'where a very wholesome beverage, strong and small, is manufactured for private use'. In addition to these, only 10·4 per cent. could even be classed as unskilled labourers, whilst agriculture claimed a mere 0·8 per cent.

Because of the unique nature of the City's employment, Bath's labour force was not subject to the normal depressions suffered by the large industries. Its people did not experience the misery of wholesale unemployment which periodically hit the textile towns of the north—nor did they live in the dread that machines would one day make them redundant. Bath had a security which few major towns could enjoy in the 1830's. The continued prosperity of its inhabitants was dependent, not on external factors of international trade, but on its continuance as a spa and social centre. As *The Bath Visitant* said in 1839: 'The trade of Bath will, as at present, be regulated for the future simply *by its own consumption*.'

Although, by that date, the aristocracy had cooled in their patronage of the city, imitators from the upper middle-class had adequately filled the gap. Bath held on to its livelihood, albeit by the skin of its teeth. It continued to consume. Trade was perhaps not quite as brisk; shopkeepers and craftsmen might pour out their grumbles at the Chartists meetings in town; but life for most was steady and comfortable. The sparkle might have left its balls and its parties; the visitors might look back nostalgically to the golden age of Nash (see Chapter Five). But Bath was still Bath for the majority of its people. The new police force and the new workhouse could cope quite easily with any drop-outs. Judging by the evidence, they were not grossly over-worked (see Chapters Three and Eight). If decline was to come, it was to come gradually. By 1841 there were signs of a creeping paralysis but the sudden seizure, which tended to strike towns involved in the industrial revolution, never came.

Of course some people inevitably suffered, even in a place like Bath, from circumstances beyond their control. But fortunately the city had a large number of charitable people who were prepared to help in such instances. The 'licensed chairman' (as the operators of the Sedan Chairs were called) were, by 1830, falling on hard times. In earlier years they had provided the vital link for Beau Nash's amusements. But the Mayor's decision in 1829 to sanction 'hackney flys' (light, horse-drawn coaches) had seriously hit their business. Mainwaring describes how the chairmen had put their case to the residents and visitors, stating 'their number to be three hundred and fifty, of whom more than two-thirds were married, with large families; that they occupied houses from ten to twenty pounds rent per annum'. Although there was some immediate response to their plea for renewed patronage, 'it could not check the progress of improvement consequent on an increased population'. The result was that some left the city in search of other jobs. Those who remained were 'unemployed half the year; and the hayfield, the harvest and other pursuits, fill up to them the vacuum of a tedious, unprofitable summer season'.[2] It is interesting to note, however, that in 1841 *The Bath Directory* still recorded the authorised fares payable for the hire of Sedan Chairs—1s. 6d. for a mile, but 6d. for three hundred yards on hills like Lansdown.

Seasonal unemployment, too, took its toll when the weather was bad. An exceptionally hard winter in 1830 caused local distress among the unskilled labourers, a fact also recorded by Mainwaring:

> Heavy and repeated falls of snow marked the beginning of this year. The ground became entirely covered to a great depth; and a severe frost setting in at the time, the customary sources of labour were entirely blocked up, and a great distress existed among the poor.

The Mayor opened a subscription list to help those who were unable to receive parish relief. £800 was collected. 'Immediate employment was, therefore, provided for more than one hundred and fifty men in clearing the streets of snow and the still more dangerous accumulation of ice, with which the pavements were everywhere encrusted. Bread, coals, blankets and (in some few urgent cases) money were distributed . . . till Providence restored to them the usual means of providing for their families, but their own honest and independent labour.'

A year later a group of wealthier citizens met at Weymouth House to establish the Bath Employment Society 'for the purpose of employing labourers belonging to the six Bath parishes, who might be thrown out of work during hard frosts in the winter season'. They were grateful and relieved to find that, whereas bad conditions elsewhere in the country had resulted in violent disturbances, 'in Bath no instance of riot or destruction of property had occurred'. Self-interest (as well as charity) told them that they should take

[2]Mainwaring: *The Annals of Bath*, pp. 318–19.

8

'advantage of our local tranquility' and prevent any future trouble by planning ahead 'for the poor, who are not able, or not in the habit of using foresight for themselves'.

Funds were raised; temporary employment was found or created. Bath was proud of its stability, its 'spirit of honest industry' and its dignified peace. Middle class traders and craftsmen, upper class residents were all prepared to invest in its preservation. Potential troublemakers were to be bought off and saved 'from that extreme destitution which makes the poor man reckless of character, a hater of the classes above him, a plunderer of his neighbour's property, a lover of disturbance'. Disturbances would be bad for trade. A reputation for riots, like oil on beaches, would keep holidaymakers away. Bath in 1831 could not afford trouble.

If stability was the keynote of Bath in the Age of Reform, what did stability mean in fact to the members of the working population? What working conditions did they possess, what standard of living did they enjoy? How did the lot of the Bath worker compare with that of his contemporaries in other cities? Did the City's affluence and air of ease rub off on the members of the lower classes? To find out the answers to these questions, a close look will be taken at two trades—millinery and dressmaking (to represent the small 'domestic' industry) and cloth-making (to represent the 'factory' side of employment).

In 1841 the *Royal Commission on the Employment of Children* sent its commissioners to Bath to compile a report which was published two years later. From the considerable number of statements taken from people involved in millinery and dressmaking at the time, a clear picture of conditions of work can be built up. This was Bath's most important single industry, employing something in the region of a thousand women.

The work itself was by no means arduous. It was largely a 'sitting-down' occupation—'but the young persons answer the bell in turns, and so get a little exercise. The rooms are comfortable, and they are never exposed to cold or damp or to excessive heat.' Each of the many dressmakers and milliners in Bath employed a team of assistants and apprentices. One business had as many as eighteen young people between the ages of sixteen and twenty-three engaged on five-year apprenticeships. This was the normal period, although some apparently managed with three years. Parents were required to pay a premium for this training. Once a girl had qualified

9

as an assistant, she would receive a salary 'varying from fifteen to forty pounds a year'.

The hours of work were long. 'They now have breakfast at seven in the morning' reported one assistant, 'and begin generally at half-past seven; and according to the business, work till eight or half-past eight or nine in the evening. But after going to London (which is done by the proprietors in the Spring for the new fashions) the hours are longer. They never, however, exceed a quarter to eleven.' These lengthy working days of between 12½ and 15¼ hours, which were typical of the trade in Bath, were at least relieved by periodical breaks. During the off-season, 'the young persons have a walk in the morning or evening, as is convenient; but for a month or two after the London fashions are working up, there is no time for this. They have breakfast, lunch, dinner, tea, and supper regularly, and with sufficient time for all; but there is not a stated portion of time allowed out for each meal.'

The general impression given by the witnesses to the Commission was that, although the hours were long, conditions were very much better in Bath than elsewhere. Several with experience complained of even longer hours in London—'from five in the morning till midnight'; 'from eight (a.m.) till two or three at night'; 'has frequently worked three nights in the week, and often on Saturday night, until nine o'clock on Sunday morning; and this without time allowed to sleep during the following days'; 'at Liverpool and other places they frequently work all night'.

The main complaint in Bath was not so much of excessive work, but of the lack of free time. One apprentice was 'altogether satisfied with her occupation, but regrets that she has not a little more time to herself'. Another, however, admitted that she 'could, if she chose, find time for walking or reading, except when the business is very urgent'. Most agreed that the job was in no way harmful to health and that 'there is no punishment or improper severity to complain of'. One, nevertheless, found the Bath climate too much, complaining 'that she suffers from langour and fatigue in the warm weather'.

Usually, the apprentices and assistants all boarded in the same house with the owners—'and are all subject to the rules and discipline of the place. The young ones are always sent to bed after supper, and, for all round, the candles are generally put out at eleven o'clock.' They were apparently well-treated and 'the inmates of the house form all, as it were, but one family'. Meals were taken together. The apprentices had, on the whole, received some education before they came. They certainly had no time to continue their studies in Bath. Nevertheless, it was common practice for them to attend Church with their master and mistress on Sundays, 'to hear a chapter of the Bible read every night' and 'say prayers night and morning daily'.

They normally had a fortnight or a month's holiday in the summer or autumn ('if their friends send for them'), together with Good Friday and a few days at Christmas. Saturday was a full working day. One dressmaker concluded by saying: 'On comparing the occupation with that of governesses and shop-women, if the hours of work were shorter and they had more exercise, they would not be badly off.' The apprentices and assistants seemed to agree with this verdict. Their life, if not exactly easy, was not oppressive. They worked in reasonable conditions for sympathetic employers.

The same would also seem to have been true of the workers at the woollen cloth factory of Messrs. Charles Wilkins & Co. at Twerton. *The Report of the Factory Commissioners* in 1833 was full of praise for the employers at Twerton:

> We had heard from the Mayor and other persons who we saw a very favourable account of the benevolent character of Mr. Wilkins, and of the constant interest he takes in the welfare of the people in his employment, and we accidently met with a proof of his kindness and indulgence towards them. His house is close by his factory, and we remarked on the lawn before his door preparations for putting up a great tent. On inquiry (but not from himself) we learned that next Monday, being Whit-Monday, he is to give dinners and various refreshments to about a thousand persons of the working classes—children and grown-up people, at different times of the day, with music and other amusements. This, moreover, we were informed, is an annual festivity on the same day. Some apology may perhaps be necessary for mentioning such a circumstance in a formal report; but as much has been said of the harshness of manufacturers towards the work-people, and of their being regardless of their comforts . . . we have thought that it would not be inappropriate to mention the fête of Mr. Wilkins as proof of that mutual kind feeling between master and workmen which we found very generally to prevail.

11

That Report together with the *House of Commons' Report on the Handloom Weavers* in 1840 enable us to construct a picture of factory conditions in the 1830's. Although it is clear that only a small proportion of the people who lived in the four main Bath parishes actually worked at the Twerton factory, the illustration will nevertheless be useful in forming an impression of local standards.

In 1833 Mr. Wilkins employed eight hundred people inside the factory plus another two or three hundred who worked in their own homes. Sixty-seven of the factory workers attended the sixty-seven power-looms, which had been installed in 1827. These were operated by two steam engines or, in case of emergency, by the more unreliable water-power of the Avon. The remainder of those employed worked more slowly at hand looms. According to the 1840 Report, the use of power-looms had 'not at any time since their introduction deprived the handloom weavers of work'. Unemployment was not a problem. 'The proprietors have great skill in the manufacture of broadcloths, and consequently the trade is flourishing, and the workmen are generally employed.'

Work conditions were good. 'The whole establishment is in a very high state of order, and although the rooms are low, we found them all well ventilated.' Although no 'medical man' was specially employed by the factory, health was satisfactory. Indeed, the only illness suffered by one worker in twenty-four years at the factory was 'a severe cold' caught at a fair. The men joined together to provide a fund for the support of the sick, paying a weekly contribution of sixpence per head. The fund was further enlarged by fines imposed on those who broke the rules of the factory.

Hours of work were inevitably long. According to Mr. Wilkins 'the average has certainly not exceeded eleven hours each day, not including Saturday, when the work is only eight hours, or sixty-three hours in the week'. The factory closed for two days' holiday at Christmas, two days at Whitsuntide, half a day at Easter, two other half days and 'one day when a dinner was given to the workpeople'. The only night work was in the fulling mill. Breaks, of course, were allowed for meals—half an hour for breakfast (from 8.30 a.m. to 9 a.m.), one hour for dinner (from 1 p.m. to 2 p.m.), half an hour for tea (from 4.30 p.m. to 5 p.m.). Most managed to go home during these intervals.

For this labour a man could earn in 1837 between 12s. and 18s. a week. Mr. Anthony Austin, the Parliamentary Commissioner, estimated that the average weekly wage for the handloom weaver in the factory was 15s. 8¼d. Even during a recent depression, they were able to earn regularly between 10s. and 15s. a week. However, because 'many of their children are employed at the factory, and their wives also when their domestic occupations will permit', the average *family* earnings in 1837 were £1 1s. 10d. per week. Austin calculated that their average living expenses per head were 5s. 0¾d. per week. The families of out-door weavers, however, were less well-off. In 1837 the average wage of a weaver working in his own home was 11s. 7½d., with only 4s. 1¼d. available per head for spending. Most of the out-door weavers were older people.

The Twerton factory, like most factories at that time, employed children—though only twenty-six under the age of nine. 'Six or seven children have been employed in these weeks at six years of age', admitted Mr. Wilkins, 'but these invariably work with their parents, are employed by them and do not work more than five to six hours per day'. He went on to defend the employment of children under twelve years of age on the grounds of 'economy on the part of the employer, the interests of the parents, and the benefit to the children themselves, by substituting habits of industry for idleness.' The older children never worked more than eleven and a half hours a day and often less in winter. 'They come about seven in the morning', said one father, 'and go away about five or six at night; but they play so much that I don't think they have more than five or six hours labour'.

The workmen assured the Commissioners in 1833 that the hours of work for children were not excessive and that they were not exhausted by their labour. 'I think that if anyone was to take a walk through the village they would be convinced of the contrary of that; the parents have hard work to bring them in from their play to go to bed.' Although they admitted that it would be nice to send children under nine to school, they also agreed that they could not afford the loss of earnings. In any case, 'the labour is so light that it does no harm to the children, either to their body or mind'. The Commissioners clearly agreed with these observations: 'We did not find one young person with an unhealthy look, and their general appearance neither indicated overwork nor scanty food. Here . . . children are all well clothed; a factory child in rags has not once met our eye.'

What worried both the employers and the Commissioners most

13

was the problem and use of the workman's leisure-time. Although the men had 'the character of being steady, sober, industrious and religious', a new temptation had recently been presented to employees both young and old. Mr. Wilkins himself complained:

> We cannot now avoid remarking, the introduction of beer-houses in this parish has been attended with the most deplorable results; children of both sexes are now habitually frequenting them, whereas before their introduction such habits were quite unknown; nor can this excite surprise, when we state there were formerly only two public-houses and two retail breweries, and directly on the passing of the Beer Bill, no less than twenty beer-shops were opened in addition to the two regular public houses . . . and we find it imposssible entirely to prevent the children and young persons in our employment from frequenting them, notwithstanding our most strenuous endeavours to do so.

Mr. Wilkins certainly did all he could to discourage his employees from becoming slaves to drink. In 1832, in order to check the growing drunkenness and absenteeism during work hours, a series of rules was drawn up with fines for offenders. Absence, negligence, and shoddy work brought penalties ranging from 1s. to 2s. 6d. (see Appendix). By 1837 the Company had turned to positive means of encouragement, seeking to provide their workmen with alternative means of filling their leisure hours. A school had been established in the factory and a reading room was being built 'which is to be warmed and lighted, and provided with suitable journals and periodicals and other books, and to be open until nine or ten o'clock at night. Tea and coffee or similar refreshments are allowed to be served here at moderate prices and the subscription will be very low'.

In the meantime, a group of senior factory workers had taken their own steps to check the growing evils of drink 'which the number of beer-houses lately opened has greatly contributed to aggravate and encourage'. They established an Association for the Promotion of Order. In the belief that 'the Sunday spent in idleness' promoted vice amongst children, the Society sought to encourage young people under twenty-one to attend public worship and Sunday School. Indeed, the firm henceforth required 'that all such in their employment shall attend public worship at least once every Sunday'. The members of the Society promised to set a good example by not drinking in a public house in Twerton on a Sunday 'except under very particular circumstances'.

Similar concern was being shown in Bath itself towards the rapid increase in drunkenness. On 6th February, 1832, a public meeting established the Temperance Society, feeling that it was impossible 'to contemplate the dreadful depravity of the lower orders in this particular vice without a sensation of horror, and an ardent desire for its removal'. 931 citizens enrolled in the Society, believing that the best weapon against vice 'is that of example'.[3]

The upper and middle classes in Bath certainly adopted a paternal attitude towards the workers. They encouraged the *industrious* poor to provide for the future in various ways. *The Bath Friendly Society*, for instance, was established in 1832 to offer insurance and security. In return for a regular subscription, a member would receive weekly payments and medical aid during times of sickness, a pension after the age of sixty-five and a sum of money at death. By the end of the first year, 250 people had joined. After ten years of existence the Society numbered 1,204 members, including the whole of the police force who, from 1838, had been obliged to enrol as a condition of their employment. Since its establishment, 2,196 members had at some time received weekly sick benefits, £989 had been paid out in addition for medical assistance and £512 to relatives on the death of members.[4]

The Repository for the Sale of Works of Industry of the Poor of Bath, on the other hand, encouraged the poor to bring for sale articles of their own work. Their professed aim was 'to associate industry with adequate remuneration'. *The East Somerset Labourers' Friendly Society* offered rewards to the best tenants of allotments, whilst the *Bath District Visiting Society* sought to encourage savings by regular visitation.[5] Clearly, the upper class worthies who formed the back-bone of these groups saw it as their duty to rescue the working classes from poverty brought about by idleness. They wanted to save not just the worker's stomach, but also his self-respect. This attitude is very much in keeping with the thinking which lay behind the setting up of the New Poor Law (see Chapter Three).

But saving money was incredibly difficult for most of the working

[3]Mainwaring: *The Annals of Bath*, pp. 383–85.
[4]*Bath Chronicle*, 16th May, 1842.
[5]Silverthorne: *Bath Directory, 1841*.

15

class population. Wages, though steady in Bath, were not excessive. Prices were high and were clearly rising. Bath Market, behind the Guildhall, was open daily for poultry, butter, vegetables and fruits; on Wednesdays and Saturdays for meat; on Mondays, Wednesdays and Fridays for fish. *The Bath Visitant* of 1839 boasted that 'The Bath markets are a proverb for cheapness, excellence of meat and cleanliness . . . Butter is brought in fresh every morning, and from its excellence is deemed one of the luxuries of Bath. No inland place is so well supplied with sea-fish as Bath'.

High quality food was certainly available—but could the Twerton textile worker in 1837 afford to buy? His average weekly earnings of 15s. 8¼d. during times of full employment would clearly not go far. But even he was much better off than the unskilled labourer who worked on Bath's roads. Between 1832 and 1839 he earned between 7s. and 9s. only a week. It is true that during the next two years his average earnings rose to just over 10s.,[6] due largely to the great demand for labour on the new Great Western Railway (see Chapter Six). But out of these wages, rent alone accounted for between 1s. 4d. and 3s. a week.[7] Much of the remainder went on food.

In December, 1837 the cheapest beef in the market[8] was 6d. per lb., fowls were 3s. 6d. each, bacon was 7d. per lb., cheese 6d. per lb., butter 10d. per lb., eggs 1d. each and bread (the staple diet) was 6½d. for a 4 lb. loaf. To gain some idea of the quantity and type of food a poor worker would eat in the course of a week, refer to the workhouse diet sheet of 1837 (page 39). It will quickly be realised that meat was a luxury and that bread, cheese and gruel formed the main ingredients. Although most of the above prices remained fairly stable during the following year, the cost of bread had risen to 9½d. by the end of 1838 (an increase of nearly a third). Wages clearly could not keep pace with dramatic increases of this kind and the poorer workers suffered terribly in consequence. It has been shown elsewhere[9] that the actual purchasing power of the labourers' wages in Bath fell considerably during the period in question. And unskilled labourers accounted for 10·4 per cent. of the City's population in the 1841 Census.

[6]*Account Books of Overseers of Highways, Walcot, 1832–41.*
[7]*Report on the Handloom Weavers, 1840.*
[8]*Bath Chronicle, 1837–38.*
[9]R. S. Neale: *The Standard of Living, 1780–1844: Economic History Review,* Vol. XIX.

With candles, soap, clothes, fuel and beer to think of in addition to food and rent, the Bath worker had little money for the so-called luxuries of life. Even the cheapest coal, which was supplied in carts from the local pits or from the canal wharf in Sydney Gardens, cost 9½d. per cwt. (excluding the cost of delivery). Gin was advertised at 10s. per imperial gallon; brandy 32s.; sauterne 50s. per dozen bottles. Hatch's Cheap Paper Hanging Warehouse in New Bond Street offered bedroom papers from 1¼d. a roll and drawing room papers from 4d. Medicine, too, was expensive. J. R. King's Drug and Patent Medicine Establishment in the Market Place provided their own Black Currant Lozenges 'for hoarseness, sore throats, loss of voice, etc.' for 1s. a box; Antibilious-Aperient pills, 'an excellent family medicine', for 1s. 1½d. a box; and Anti-Scorbutic dentifrice 'for cleansing and preserving the teeth and gums' for 1s. 1½d. box. Health, it seems, was a preserve of the rich. A visit to London by coach (in eleven or twelve hours) would cost £2 inside and 18s. outside.[10] All of these experiences, however, were clearly outside the scope of the working classes.

How far did the workers of Bath accept their lot in this Age of Reform? What measures did they take to improve their standard of living? Were they involved in any of the national protest movements of this time? There is little to suggest that the outburst of trade unionism at the start of the 1830's had any great or violent repercussion in the City of Bath—although a variety of trade clubs did exist. Indeed, Mainwaring in 1832 referred to the trade unions which had been formed in London 'for the purpose of intimidating and compelling masters to submit to exorbitant payments for the services of their journeymen'—but added that 'the effects of those combinations were but slightly felt in this city'.[11] Nevertheless, when the crowds of ordinary Bath people who had demonstrated in favour of parliamentary reform in 1832 (see Chapter Two) found that they had been cheated, they were quick to join in the popular movements which gained force towards the close of the 1830's. The most important amongst these were the Chartist Movement and the Anti-Corn Law League.

The Chartist Movement, which had its origins in William Lovett's London Working Man's Association of 1836, advocated substantial electoral reform, including manhood suffrage. The Movement

[10]Silverthorne: *The Bath Directory, 1837.*
[11]Mainwaring: *The Annals of Bath*, p. 453.

eventually became very strong in the area around Bath. Social decline in Bath itself and economic decline in the neighbouring cloth towns of Frome, Bradford-on-Avon and Trowbridge saw to it that there were plenty of disgruntled workers and traders. A Working Man's Association was therefore established in Bath as early as 1837 and started to agitate not only for parliamentary reform, but also against the purely local grievances—the new workhouse, the new police force, the new City Council. These working-class reformers (led by the Bartlett brothers) were soon joined by middle-class radicals (led by Alderman James Crisp).

The Bath Chartists held regular meetings (weekly by 1841) and processions; supported the National Petition to Parliament; sent a representative to the national Convention of 1839; and agreed to support the idea of a 'Sacred Month' (or strike) if the Petition should be rejected. But although the Bath Chartists were enthusiastic and bombarded the inhabitants with forthright posters, they were never as active or as menacing as those in the neighbouring Wiltshire towns. There torchlight processions, violent speeches, armed gatherings and arrests were all quite frequent. In Bath the authorities, with their regular police force, were more watchful and more prepared. A large Chartist meeting planned for Whit Monday, 1839 was a flop, largely because the Lord Mayor, whose confidence was re-inforced by the presence of regular troops, refused to allow it to take place inside the City. Few turned up to the new site at Midford. Similarly, the police sent spies into a private meeting of Chartists held in their Monmouth Street headquarters and arrested three of their leaders on charges of sedition.[12]

Nevertheless, by 1841 the Chartists had gained a considerable following in the City and were seeking hard to win over other liberal groups to their cause (see Appendix). The Anti-Corn Law League was one such group. This had been founded in 1839 by Cobden and Bright to gain the repeal of the Corn Laws (1815), which sought to restrict the entry of foreign corn to this country. In Bath middle-class liberals, like Admiral Gordon and ex-Mayor, William Hunt, largely supported the League. Meetings were held in which they blamed the Corn Laws for distress in the towns and argued that their abolition would reduce the ever-rising price of bread.[13]

The Bath Tories, on the other hand, rejected these arguments in

[12]R. B. Pugh: *Chartism in Somerset and Wiltshire* (in Briggs: *Chartist Studies*).
[13]*Bath Chronicle*, 23rd December, 1841.

18

a series of posters and through the editorial columns of the *Bath Chronicle*. Their main theme was that repeal of the Corn Laws would lead to unemployment on the land as foreign corn flooded the markets and a general lowering of wages. The following poster expressed their views clearly:

CHEAP BREAD AND LOW WAGES

An Irishman was asked at a shop in London sixpence for four eggs. 'Why, in Mayo', he exclaimed, 'I could have had two dozen for sixpence'. 'And why,' he was asked, 'did you not stop in Mayo, since you could buy things so cheaply there?' 'Because,' he replied, 'I could not get the sixpences to buy them with!'

'This little anecdote applies equally well to the Repeal of the Corn Laws, which would reduce the price of the Quartern loaf, but would take away the sixpences which now enable you to buy it'.

Bath was divided on the Corn Laws—but the Chartists tried hard to enlist the help of the League. A most unusual joint meeting of the two groups was held on 20th December, 1841 in the Guildhall for the purpose of petitioning Parliament for the total repeal of the Corn Laws, and in support of the People's Charter! Although the Chartists were quick to refer to this 'happy union of the Chartists and the middle-classes', the *Chronicle* claimed that 'eight tenths of the persons in the room belonged exclusively to the working-classes' and that the others had only come out of 'curiosity'. Both sides addressed the meeting. Vincent spoke for the Chartists:

The Corn Law, he declared, would continue until the Corn-Law League came over to the Chartists and declared for a full, fair and entire representation of the people. He recommended the getting up of such an agitation as would frighten the aristocracy into the granting of the people's demands. He called upon the middle-classes to fraternize with the Chartists...[14]

Such was working class feeling in Bath. Chartism and the League gave them their opportunity to speak out against their conditions and against the changes which had swept them into the Age of Reform. They were vociferous, but not violent. Their hardship, cushioned by the sympathy of their betters and the stability of the City's economy, was not after all intolerable.

[14]*Bath Chronicle*, 23rd December, 1841.

Sources

The Census Returns, 1841 (Public Record Office).
Royal Commission's Report on the Employment of Children, 1843 (British Museum H.C. (1843) Vol. IV).
Report of the Factory Commission, 1833 (British Museum, H.C. 1833).
Report on the Handloom Weavers, 1840 (British Museum, H.C. (1840) Vol. XXIII).
Account Books of the Overseers of the Highways, Walcot, 1832–41 (Bath Reference Library).
Two Scrapbooks of Newscuttings, Broadsheets and Small Posters relating to Bath Affairs (Bath Reference Library).
R. Mainwaring: *The Annals of Bath, 1838.*
H. Silverthorne: *The Bath Directory, 1837; 1841.*
G. S. Gibbes: *The Bath Visitant, 1839.*
G. S. Gibbes: *The New Bath Guide, 1834.*
Bath Chronicle.
R. S. Neale: *The Standard of Living, 1780–1844:* a Regional Class Study (in *The Economic History Review*, Vol. XIX).
R. B. Pugh: *Chartism in Somerset and Wiltshire* (in Asa Briggs: *Chartist Studies* (1967)).

CHAPTER TWO

Bath and the Great Reform Bill

Stephen Brooks

BEFORE the passing of the Great Reform Bill in 1832, Bath was a 'rotten borough', suffering under a form of electoral injustice established over a century before when Parliament had decreed that only the corporation, a self-perpetuating oligarchy, should have the right to vote in the election of Bath's two Members of Parliament. Consequently, in 1830 only thirty of Bath's population of some 50,000 could vote.

Nevertheless, the people of Bath were not apathetic towards politics, and in 1830, when the day for the election arrived—it was 1st July—a large crowd gathered by ten o'clock in front of the Guildhall. Since there were only thirty electors it was a simple matter to use bribes and threats to sway their votes, so it was wealth and personal influence which carried most weight in elections. In 1830 there were three candidates: Lord John Thynne, the brother of the Marquis of Bath, Lord Brecknock, who was the Marquis of Camden's son, and General Charles Palmer, a leading citizen of Bath but also a popular liberal. When the doors of the Guildhall were opened the people rushed in, cheering Palmer, ignoring Thynne and jeering at Brecknock who was highly unpopular.[1] The votes of the corporation were taken by a show of hands, and the mayor delared Lord John Thynne and General Palmer to have been duly elected: the crowd were jubilant. Then followed the high spot of the election for the onlookers, the 'chairing' of the members, when the victors were carried round the city on gold and crimson velvet

---

[1]General Palmer had first been elected as M.P. for Bath in 1808 as the nominee of the Marquis of Camden. Later he quarrelled with Lord Camden, who in 1826 put up his son, Lord Brecknock, to oppose the General. Brecknock succeeded in defeating Palmer, hence his unpopularity.

chairs in the riotous manner portrayed by Hogarth. With the two members at its head, the procession moved off up Union Street and Milsom Street, along George Street, up Gay Street and through the Circus to General Palmer's house in Brock Street. All the streets were colourfully decorated and the people waved banners from their windows. During the procession, the successful candidates distributed silver and tickets for over six hundred gallons of beer which could be 'cashed' at local public houses. Voteless or not, it was evidently still thought wise to be on good terms with the crowd.

Such was the farce which was called an election before the Great Reform Act, but even prior to 1832, the narrow limits of the franchise had not gone unchallenged. In October 1812 on election day John Allen, a well-known Bathonian, stood up and demanded that the freemen of the city should also be allowed to vote. What justification he thought he had for this is not recorded, but the Mayor and corporation thought he had none and ignored him, continuing with the established voting procedure. Very annoyed, Mr. Allen went outside and proceeded to hold his own election, collecting some twenty-eight votes from freemen assembled to await the outcome of their case. The next day Mr. Allen arrived at the Guildhall at eleven o'clock to continue with his 'mock election' and started to address the large crowd which had gathered. By one account a body of constables then rushed out of the Guildhall and tried to drag the trouble-maker back inside, but Mr. Allen was defended by the crowd with such vigour that not only were the constables forced to beat a hasty retreat but the outside of the Guildhall was also badly damaged. It was only after the Mayor had read the riot act and six arrests had been made that the mob dispersed. Those responsible for the disorder were strongly condemned by one writer, whose attack was principally motivated by sympathy for the poor landladies of the city: 'Will not the reports of these disorders, ever exaggerated, tend to protract the arrival of visitants in Bath and thus materially injure the early part of the season?' Clearly an early instance of Bath's concern for its 'tourist trade'.

It was not until the era of violence and disorder harshly suppressed by the government at the end of the Napoleonic Wars had given way to more settled and prosperous times that parliamentary reform was again discussed in Bath. But the climate of opinion was certainly changing. In the general election which followed the rejection of the Whigs' first Reform Bill in April 1831, when the Prime Minister,

Lord Grey, appealed to the country, a speaker at Bath declared that 'it could never be contended that thirty men should possess the exclusive rights of returning members for this large and opulent city.' The voice of common sense seemed to prevail at last in Bath and in the country as a whole: the Whigs were returned with a majority of over a hundred. The radicals of Bath showed their growing impatience with the symbols of the old order in the course of the chairing of the members in the election of May 1831, when, according to one witness, 'the fair limits of electioneering freedom were exceeded', and the unfortunate Lord John Thynne was pelted with so much rotten fruit that he had to retreat into the White Hart,[2] leaving General Palmer to enjoy the triumphal procession alone.

There was great indignation in Bath when the Lords rejected a second Reform Bill after it had passed the Commons on 7th October, 1831. 'The intelligence reached this city in the afternoon of 8th October and was generally received with feelings of the deepest regret.' A meeting was therefore held on Thursday, 13th October, to show the Lords what the people of Bath thought of their conduct. It began with a procession down Pulteney Street with bands playing and banners supporting the Whig government, and then 20,000 people gathered in front of the Sydney Hotel[3] to hear the speeches in favour of reform. It was a striking, and a peaceful, demonstration and the many that took place all over the country must have impressed the Lords with the strength of the nation's wish for reform, and hastened their decision to hold it up no longer.

Not all demonstrations were so peaceful, and serious rioting took place in Bristol on Saturday, 29th October, and again on the Sunday, until on Monday troops were called in to clear the streets; sixty-four people were injured. Reports quickly reached Bath and on the Sunday evening a large crowd of ruffians gathered outside the White Hart to hear the latest news from Bristol. What had all the makings of a serious incident then occurred, when Captain Wilkins of the Bath troop of Yeomanry Cavalry going to Bristol to help quell the riots, arrived in Bath to collect his men and unwisely stopped at the White Hart. The hostile crowd jostled him as he went into the inn and after breaking all the windows, tried to follow him inside. But the inn-keeper was fortunately well-prepared and 'red-hot

---

[2] This inn was on the site opposite the colonnade at the end of the Abbey Churchyard where the Grand Pump Room Hotel formerly stood.
[3] Now the Holburne of Menstrie Museum.

kitchen pokers, previously prepared, had an admirable effect in causing the assailing party to turn round and beat a hasty retreat'. The quick thinking of the landlord of the White Hart saved the immediate situation, until about three hundred special constables were sworn in to clear the streets. On the Monday morning people 'of all grades of respectability in society' crowded to the Guildhall to enrol as special constables, and 'to the great pride of the citizens, not the slightest attempts at any renewal of disturbances occurred'. A grim postscript can be added to the events of Sunday evening: three of those arrested outside the White Hart were sentenced to death, and only at the last moment were their sentences commuted to transportation for life.

Bath was therefore, spared the worst of the riots which followed the Lords' rejection of the second Reform Bill. But the demonstrations throughout the country and the King's promise to Lord Grey to create as many Whig Lords as were necessary to ensure a majority favourable to reform in the upper house, forced the Lords to back down: in June 1832, the Great Reform Act became law. The news was greeted with great jubilation in Bath, and a 'Grand Reform Gala' with acrobats and fireworks was held in the Sydney Gardens as an official celebration. Processions, banquets and parties were all held in the next few weeks as Bath rejoiced with the rest of the nation at the victory of the new over the old. But though it was a victory, it was not a rout: changes in the franchise for instance, were not as sweeping as many radicals had hoped. To ensure that all electors were responsible men with a 'stake in the community', the vote in boroughs was only given to adult males who occupied houses of an annual rateable value of £10 or over. Since this was quite a high figure, in Bath at least it qualified only 3,000 people to vote out of the population of 50,000: the last thing the Whig government intended to do was to bring about a 'democracy'.

December 1832 was fixed as the date for the first trial by general election of the new system. Candidates were not slow in coming forward to stand for the privilege of representing Bath in the first reformed parliament. Lord John Thynne and the Earl of Brecknock stood aside, aware at least that they belonged to the old and were not wanted in the new, but General Palmer announced that he would once again be standing. Since there were no party organisations in 1832, each candidate was responsible for announcing his intention to stand, and forming a committee to manage his campaign. So in the *Bath Chronicle* of 21st June appeared the following letter, addressed to 'The Independent Electors of Bath':

Gentlemen, I take the earliest opportunity of respectfully announcing my intention to offer myself as a candidate for your suffrages on the next dissolution of parliament.

And it was signed Henry William Hobhouse. At the same time an announcement appeared that Mr. Hobhouse's election committee would meet on Mondays and Fridays at eleven o'clock at the White Lion to see potential supporters. In his preliminary statements Mr. Hobhouse declared his principles to be in line with those of Lord Grey's government which had passed the Reform Bill. However, when, on 2nd July, he held his first meeting at the Masonic Hall in the parish of St. James,[4] many radicals considered that his views on reform were far too lukewarm, so much so that they felt a third candidate was essential. This view was not universal though, for the *Bath Chronicle* was firmly convinced that Mr. Hobhouse's showing at the Masonic Hall was well calculated to give satisfaction to the majority of reformers! The rumours of a third candidate gave rise to an editorial on 30th August warning against 'unnecessary upstirrings of political sentiment'.

Nevertheless, on 13th September a meeting was held in the Upper Assembly Rooms[5] to 'introduce Mr. John Roebuck to the Electors of Bath'. Some citizens of Bath had written to Joseph Hume, a distinguished radical, asking him to recommend someone with similar opinions to his own, and he had nominated John Roebuck. The arrival of this new candidate on the scene was greeted with some disapproval, especially since only on 10th September, Robert Blake Foster of Lansdown Crescent had offered to stand so that the 'rank, wealth and worth of Bath should not be totally unrepresented', or, in other words, as a Tory. With these developments, the election campaign in Bath hit the national headlines. In *The Times* of 17th September it was stated, 'there is another mischief besetting the reform interest and that is internal division: Bath seems to be a case in point'. On 22nd September *The Times* thundered:

It ought to be recollected that an elective battle between two or more members of the liberal party may end, not merely in the

[4]Situated in York Street—now the Friends' Meeting House.
[5]Situated off the Circus.

25

defeat of one of them but in the triumph of the common enemy over both.

This challenge was taken up by *The Examiner* on 30th September. Mr. Foster, it declares, only stood from an 'idle love of notoriety . . . His share of the contest is the burlesque part of the scene'. So there was no fear of his getting elected; indeed on 31st October he withdrew his candidature. No, the real contest was between Roebuck and Hobhouse, for the latter was really a Tory in disguise, supported by Bath's Tory corporation. It is fair to remark that Mr. Hobhouse was probably only supported by them for want of a serious more conservative candidate, but it was not an association which could do him much good when 'Tory' was an approbrious word.

So by the middle of September all the contenders were in the field. General Palmer was confident of his election on his past merits and long service to Bath, and could remain largely aloof from the hectic business of electioneering; so this left John Roebuck and Henry Hobhouse fighting it out for the other seat. The system of political parties as we know it today had no place in 1832: indeed, party was equated with selfishness and faction, and near polling day the people of Bath were urged to rise above 'every sordid and mean and party consideration'. Each candidate had therefore, to make known his own personal opinions to the electors without reference to any 'party manifesto'. None of the candidates regarded themselves as party men; General Palmer on several occasions insisted on his independence of any other individual or group: it was his own personality and principles which would secure election not adherence to a party. Mr. Hobhouse too only intended to give a general guide to his principles when he identified them with those of Lord Grey's government. The practice (until recently) of putting only a candidate's name on a ballot paper, not his party, would have been more valid in 1832 than it is today.

But ballot papers were unheard of in 1832, for one of the injustices of the old system, open and public voting, still remained, giving ample opportunity for intimidation and corruption. This was a recognised fact for the Mayor warned at the beginning of the election in December, 'I trust particularly that free access to the places of polling will be found by even the most timid voter'. Though many Tories declared that secret voting was 'un-English', the demand for a secret ballot was one of the major issues at the election, and all the candidates spoke in favour of it.

Fig. 1   Entrance to Bath from the south side of the Old Bridge

Fig. 2   Bond Street with portraits of Bath swells

Fig. 3   Milsom Street

Fig. 4   The Market Place, Bath

Fig. 5   Walcot Church from Guinea Lane

Fig. 6   Holloway, Bath

Fig. 7   Fire at Bath at Butcher's Tallow Chandler, Saw Close

Fig. 8   View of Bath from the Lower Bristol Road

At a time of such great political upheaval, there were naturally a large number of outstanding national issues to be debated. On many of these the candidates differed, for Mr. Hobhouse took a much more moderate and cautious line than Mr. Roebuck. On the question of slavery, for instance, one of the burning issues of the day, Mr. Roebuck was for its immediate and total abolition. Mr. Hobhouse, on the other hand declared on 16th July that 'a partial abolition should be made at once and be continued on such a scale as not to risk the welfare of the slave or the planter'. As in every election today, taxation was another key issue. Mr. Hobhouse maintained that taxation could not be avoided, but he was in favour of a shift in the main burden from indirect taxation to a new property tax. For Mr. Roebuck's side, however, such a reorganisation did not get right to the heart of the problem. Basically, taxation was far too high for them, for if sinecures were abolished and the armed forces reduced, the revenue necessary for the state from taxation could be halved. As a result of the debates on the various issues, many radicals declared that though Mr. Hobhouse claimed to be a reformer, he was not, as *The Examiner* put it, 'a reformer of the stamp they desired'.

The question of public expenditure and taxation gave rise to one of the most heated personal controversies of the election, when Mr. Roebuck's supporters accused Mr. Hobhouse of hypocrisy in his views on making taxation fairer, since members of his own family were helping to increase it by accepting sinecures and pensions from the government. This was hotly denied by the Hobhouse camp, and statement upon statement appeared as one accusation and refutation followed another. Yet Mr. Roebuck himself was not free from attack, for when personalities counted for so much there was a great deal to be said for blackening your opponent's character. At one point Mr. Roebuck was accused of being a wild republican extremist, born in America and aged only twenty-five, not the sort to be sent to Parliament. These charges were strongly denied in a handbill which gave Mr. Roebuck's age as 30 and his nationality as British (he was, in fact, born in India in 1801 and lived in Canada until he was twenty-three) and at a meeting on 20th September, he made a special point of denying that he was a republican: 'with an independent commons with interest the same as the Nations, the retention of the Monarchy and Lords is quite acceptable.' Some considerable ill-feeling was created by these attacks, and at the large

27

gathering for the nomination of members on 10th December, Mr. Roebuck demanded that his opponent disown the members of his committee responsible for all the libels. Mr. Hobhouse in his turn, declared sadly:

I have made my way in this campaign as best I could through mistakes, misrepresentations and slanders, quite unprecedented in electioneering welfare.

A completely new problem for nearly all parliamentary candidates in the first election after the Great Reform Act was making themselves and their opinions known to a whole mass of eager new voters. In Bath posters were displayed all over the city and thousands of leaflets were distributed, but public meetings were the mainstay of the campaign. Mr. Roebuck, for instance, held a meeting in St. James' parish on 17th September; on 18th September he met the electors of the parish of Walcot at the tennis courts; and on 23rd September 3,000 people heard him speak in the Sydney Gardens. Though Mr. Hobhouse was fortunate in having the *Bath Chronicle* on his side, he suffered from the great handicap of not enjoying public meetings. During his very first meeting on 2nd July, he was shouted down by a group of noisy radicals and this happened all too frequently. Mr. Roebuck on the other hand was quite at ease before a mass audience and made capital out of any interruptions. When hissed at by one of the audience on nomination day he retorted, 'as you can tell which way the wind blows by a straw so you can sometimes tell which way the serpent lies by his hiss', which was greeted with great approval by the crowd.

Hobhouse probably felt more at ease in the relaxed atmosphere of a dinner such as the one he gave on 12th September, which about 250 people attended. It was certainly a great success for Mr. Hobhouse, but it gave the radicals yet another opportunity to attack him. For the charge of the dinner, provided 'in excellent style by Mr. Fortt', was only ten shillings per head, which the radicals claimed could not possibly cover the real cost, and was therefore an attempt to bribe the voters who attended. Though there was no limit on the amount a candidate could spend on his campaign, there was a great deal of hostility in Bath to the thought that money might corrupt the fair choice of members for the first reformed parliament.

The electors of Bath were determined to exercise their right to vote very carefully, and showed a certain suspicion of politicians not unknown today. This was demonstrated by the insistence during the campaign that the two new candidates should give pledges on what they would do if elected, and by the radical demand voiced by Mr. Roebuck for general elections every three, instead of every seven years, so that the politicians could be called to account more frequently. There was some dispute over the value of pledges. At Mr. Hobhouse's meeting in St. James' Parish, he declared that he favoured the repeal of the Septennial Act, but so that the Tories would not be able to complain: 'Here we have reform again—always reform', the matter should be temporarily shelved. When one of the audience, Mr. Crisp, urged him to pledge his support, if elected, in the next session of parliament for the repeal of the Act, Mr. Hobhouse maintained it was unfair to try and bind a candidate by pledges because circumstances changed so quickly: 'If I am to be trusted there is no occasion for me to be pledged and if you cannot trust me, do not send me.' That was the end of the matter as far as Mr. Hobhouse was concerned, but many voters must have taken note of his final remarks, feeling that without pledges they were at the mercy of any unscrupulous politician who chose to take advantage of their rather limited political experience.

The campaign, of course, did have its lighter side, for the amateur satirists of the day could not resist taking part. Posters, for instance, appeared round Bath announcing the arrival of Mr. Henry Van Hobson Housen with his 'Tory menagerie', containing a number of 'useless and disagreeable animals'. As a sequel to this, another poster appeared stating that because of the 'intolerable stench arising from some of the reptiles in the menagerie, Mr. Van Hobson Housen intends to dispose of them by public auction', including such beasts as the 'Thick Skullis Jobio Salyo, an amphibious animal, noted only for stupidity and dirty tricks'. Mr. J. L. Seale, one of Mr. Hobhouses's committee, can have been scarcely amused!

While the ballyhoo of electioneering was going on, careful work was being done behind the scenes to get everything ready for the actual election, for having an electorate of 3,000 instead of 30 as previously, presented no small administrative problem. Firstly, an official roll of those eligible to vote had to be completed. Provisional lists were pinned up round the town, so that anyone who felt he had been unfairly omitted could appeal to 'Wake, Smirke and Coleridge, barristers', who presided at the White Lion[6] on 18th and 19th

[6]Next to the Guildhall.

October to hear complaints. Some 200 were allowed and the names were added to the roll. Not all were lucky: a coloured man had his appeal disallowed because he was born at the Cape of Good Hope in 1793, four years too soon, as England did not capture the colony until 1797, and he did not therefore qualify as British. The biggest problem was how the actual polling was to be done. This was solved by arranging for it to take place over two days at polling stations, one for each of five of Bath's parishes, and three for the parish of Walcot; the people in the parish of Lyncombe and Widcombe, for instance, were to declare their votes at the poor house in Claverton Street. Thanks to the planning done by the Mayor and his officials, the voting went off without any difficulties, and over the two days, over 80 per cent. of those registered made their appearance at their respective polling stations to declare their votes.

Monday, 10th December was the day fixed for the official nomination of the candidates. A hustings was erected in Orange Grove and by eleven o'clock a crowd of some 7,000 had gathered. The Mayor, William Clark, arrived with the three candidates, Palmer, Hobhouse and Roebuck, and after he had appealed for there to be 'no breach of the public tranquility' during the course of the election, each of the candidates was proposed and seconded in turn. Then in a strange throw-back to pre-Reform Act days:

> The mayor then put the question to the electors, and on a show of hands declared the election to have fallen on General Palmer and Mr. Roebuck. His worship then announced that a poll was demanded on the part of Mr. Hobhouse and that voting would commence on Wednesday morning at nine o'clock.

The Mayor's appeal was respected, and no disorder is reported to have occurred throughout Wednesday, 12th and Thursday, 13th December. By the close of the poll at four o'clock on Wednesday the voting figures were as follows: Palmer, 1,039, Roebuck, 861, and Hobhouse 807. The *Bath Chronicle*, as optimistic as it was partisan, declared that 'the result of the first day's polling . . . has nothing to do with the final issue of the election'. Voting continued on Thursday, and then on Friday morning Orange Grove became the scene for the final act of the election, the declaration of the poll. The mayor arrived solemnly at ten o'clock with the thirteen poll books and invited the crowd to 'amuse themselves by telling stories to each other' while he totalled up the votes. A whole hour passed before the Mayor stepped forward to speak:

I have carefully cast up the voters in the poll books and I find that the number of votes recorded in favour of General Palmer is 1,492, and of Mr. Roebuck 1,138, and of Mr. Hobhouse 1,040, and the majority of votes having fallen on Major-General Charles Palmer and on John Arthur Roebuck, I declare those gentlemen to be duly elected, and I proclaim them to be your representatives in parliament.

The audience erupted into wild cheering, and the two victorious candidates were taken off in a carriage to tour the city followed by a great crowd of triumphant citizens. It was, as Mr. Roebuck said, 'a mighty victory indeed'.

By showing that reform was not synonymous with revolution, the events of 1832 became a landmark in English political history; and the people of Bath could well—and indeed did—congratulate themselves that they had played their part with a due sense of the responsibility which rested on them in the first election under the new system. As General Palmer and Mr. Roebuck acknowledged the cheering crowds in the streets of Bath, they could scarcely have foreseen how short-lived was to be the triumph of the 'reform interest'. Soon a reaction set in against the incapacity and radical leanings of the Whig government. Bath, sharing in this reaction, repented of its brief affair with radicalism, and in the General Election of 1837 both General Charles Palmer and John Arthur Roebuck failed to win re-election.[7]

[7] At the time Mr. Roebuck contended that his defeat at the polls in what became known as the 'Drunken Election of 1837' was due to 'Tory gold, Tory intimidation and Whig duplicity'. The argument that there was not a genuine shift of opinion to the right in Bath in 1837, as Mr. Roebuck would have claimed, is supported by the fact that in 1841 he regained his seat at Bath, although in the rest of the country there was a strong swing to the Conservatives which brought in Peel's ministry.

Sources

Thomas Falconer: *The Bath Election, 1832: A Collection of Posters, Broadsides, Pamphlets etc.* (Bath Reference Library).
Bath Chronicle.
R. Mainwaring: *The Annals of Bath, 1838.*

31

CHAPTER THREE

Bath and the New Poor Law

STEPHEN WILLIAMS

A DISCUSSION of the impact of a nationally-important measure on a local area ought to include mention of economic factors distinguishing that area. As these have received a detailed treatment in Chapter One, we shall forego repetition, pausing only to make the two general points: that Bath workers, like most workers nationally, were suffering from rising prices; but that owing to Bath's status as a resort and the diversity of employment, their work was less likely to be subject to slumps than, say, in the surrounding textile areas, and that therefore poverty was less of a problem in Bath than elsewhere.

Prior to the 1834 Amendment Act, the provisions for the relief of the poor had been dictated by the Elizabethan Poor Law. Under this system, money or goods could be supplied to the destitute in their own homes, and this was known as 'outdoor relief'. But those who, it was felt, were undeserving cases—because of their idleness or degeneracy—were often only given so called 'indoor relief', that is, they were forced to enter a poorhouse. The unit of local administration of the Poor Law was the parish, and the proportion of outdoor relief to indoor relief given varied from parish to parish—in many cases a parish could not afford to run a poorhouse. With the vast industrial change beginning during the eighteenth century the system began to creak at the seams. The parish rates necessary to pay for the relief became prohibitively high. A temporary industrial recession could create havoc with a parish's finances. In desperation such parishes enforced settlement orders on persons becoming chargeable on the rates, that is, paupers not born in their parish of residence were removed to their parish of birth, to be relieved there.

32

And this inhumane practice became widespread. After 1834 the old system, outmoded though it had been by the industrial revolution, was remembered as a paupers' golden age of understanding and sympathy, instead of the cold hearts and tight wads of the present Guardians. But these were the rosy tints of retrospection. The Old Poor Law was most often a grudging concession of bare subsistence for the utterly helpless.

In Bath, for example, in 1814, the Walcot parish overseers set up the Morford Street pin-factory, with a pauper labour-force, so as to gain some financial return from about 100 children who were burdening the parish rates. To avoid expense, between 1800 and 1820 at least 139 persons and their families were removed under settlement orders from St. James' Parish. For those who were not entitled to benefit from the system, the situation was grim indeed. Conditions in the privately run poorhouse[1] were anything but ideal, in spite of the immense finance behind it:

> . . . sick persons were not separated from those in health and in a few instances were lying in the same beds. The House is unfit for the purpose. The situation is subject to inundations. The rooms generally very low. The hall in which 100 to near 150 persons ought to spend their day and eat their meals is about 25 feet in length, 17 feet wide and 7½ feet in height consequently the greatest part of the inmates are obliged to spend their lives and eat their meals in their sleeping rooms, by which they become offensive.

Abusive or disorderly paupers were locked in the Strong Room on bread and water. In 1804 and again in 1812 a Master of the House had to be dismissed for improper treatment of the paupers; and paupers were never allowed to leave the House.[2]

Yet times were hard enough, and pauperism attractive enough, for no less than 16 per cent. of Walcot parish to be on poor relief in 1820.[3] This was because paupers, if they did not go into the poorhouse—and clearly not all of them could—were entitled to receive 'out-relief', that is, direct gifts of money and goods from the parish.

[1]There were three poorhouses in Bath before 1834—the Walcot Poorhouse (at the back of Weymouth Street), the Lyncombe and Widcombe Poorhouse (at the back of Claverton Street) and the Poorhouse run by the parish of St. Peter and St. Paul.

[2]Poor Law Committee Book, St. Peter and St. Paul, 1784–1812.

[3]*Bath and Cheltenham Gazette*, 25th April, 1821.

But pauperism of this extent, never envisaged by the Elizabethan Poor Law, increased the parish rates on the poor but independent labourer until they became oppressive. The case was cited, in a pamphlet[4] written by one of the new Guardians, of a man who, being out of work through illness, fled to his home parish Weston, from his home in Bridport because he had 4s. 10d. to pay in rates there. In fact, it was generally true that when legal action was necessary to get the rates, it was usually for a few shillings.

There is some evidence moreover that this unwilling sacrifice, the poor rate, was abused. The same pamphleteer mentions certain examples of what he calls 'pauper arrogance', and his theme is that paupers receiving out-relief were being unnecessarily pampered. He mentions the old man who boasted of spending £40 of parish money on tobacco through the years. He recalls the man who refused a request by the parish to maintain his mother (it was normal procedure to expect relatives of paupers to support them) but left a standing order for her in a local gin-shop. These examples probably do not have any general significance, but they show the way some of the Guardians were thinking in 1836. In fact, the out-paupers were not solely dependent upon relatives and the parish. Always a charitable city, Bath threw up fourteen charitable societies between 1790 and 1811, some of which were wealthy and well-organised. The Bath Employment Society, for example, was finding work in the difficult year of 1831 for 354 men at 6s. to 8s. per week (see Chapter One).

This was the situation when the Poor Law Amendment Act was passed in 1834. The Act recognised one of the urgent needs we have hinted at, namely, to make the Poor Law administration more centralized and more efficient. The whole system came under the control of three poor-law commissioners and their secretary ('iron man' Edwin Chadwick) based on Somerset House in London. Yet more important, parishes were grouped into 'Unions' to administer workhouses. The Unions were to be controlled by boards of Guardians—elected by the ratepayers. The other important provisions of the act were directed against the pauper and, it was thought in favour of the ratepayer: there was to be no outdoor relief except for the sick and aged, that is, all able-bodied poor were to be relieved only inside workhouses; and workhouse conditions should be 'less

4Spencer: *The New Poor Law: Its Evils and their remedies.*

34

eligible' (or less desirable) than the conditions of the poorest worker outside them.

It was with these directives that in 1836, the Board of Guardians, with 41 members elected from each parish and eight ex-officio members, was set up to administer the Poor Law in Bath. From the start it showed itself to be infused with a Benthamite utilitarian ideology, which regarded poverty as a personal failure of the pauper: '. . . pauperism, like drunkenness, is a habit from which a person is scarcely ever recovered'.[5] It drew a clear distinction between the incapable and the rest—who were assumed to be idle. A motion in the *Guardians' Minute Book* gives definitive utterance to the Board's philosophy: 'that the workhouse ought to be considered a house of industry for the able-bodied and a test for the idle; but that it ought to be regarded only as an asylum for the aged and infirm and as such conducted on more lenient principles'.[6] Its most basic economic mistake was its assumption that employment is always available for those who want it, from which it deduced conclusions like: '. . . on the most careful inquiry and on the most moderate calculation, three-fourths of pauperism may be attributed to this habit of drinking'.[7] Its most basic human mistake was contempt for paupers: 'while 8s. paid to the independent labourer will bring his master 10s., 5s. to the pauper labourer will bring his master 2s. 6d.'[8] But it is important to remember that, foreign as it seems to the humanitarian twentieth century, these ideas were common in the nineteenth century and not an invention of the Poor Law Amendment Act: so that even in 1821 there is a distinctly gloating tone in the overseers' report which reads: 'for we made it a rule never to give relief but by work (except in the case of sickness, extreme old age and infancy) . . . and two or three days is in general the longest time we have to employ them, before they quit and provide for themselves.'[9]

On this ideological foundation, the regulations of the Board were erected. Able-bodied paupers, it had been directed, were to be relieved only inside the workhouse, and in 1837, it was reported that there were 1,000 paupers in Walcot workhouse, 'but hardly any able-bodied males. They are mostly widows, or mothers of illegitimate

[5]Spencer: *The Failure of the New Poor Law in the Bath Union.*
[6]*Minute Book of the Board of Guardians, 1838–39,* p. 78.
[7]Spencer: *The New Poor Law.*
[8]*Bath and Cheltenham Gazette,* 28th February, 1837.
[9]*Bath and Cheltenham Gazette,* 25th April, 1821.

children who were exceedingly depraved and resentful'.[10] Even the aged and infirm paupers were sent into the workhouse if the Relieving Officer reported them to be of bad character. It was agreed that any relief to able-bodied paupers was 'furnished by way of loan', and later the principle was recognised that 'a pauper funeral should be marked and different from that of the independent poor'.[11] So punishment for their criminal poverty reached them even beyond the grave.

Granted that the Board had some basically misguided principles, it is also true that its administrative ability was immensely superior to the old parochial system. In the first place, regular attendance was guaranteed, contrary to the custom of the old vestry committees. The St. Peter and Paul committee book shows that, for example, there were no meetings between 3rd October, 1809 and 10th April, 1810 owing to several occasions on which there were insufficient numbers to make up a quorum. Unlike the old committees also, the Board had an experienced, full-time clerk to transact its business. Through him, as he was a member of the Union Clerks Association —designed for 'the free interchange of such proceedings in their district as may be of general importance'—the Board could gain a more accurate picture of legal complications in the Poor Law. The running of the workhouse was no longer the responsibility of private contractors—who clearly sought profits at the expense of either the paupers or the ratepayers—but that of salaried officials, who were moreover under the direct aegis of a committee of Guardians who inspected the workhouse twice every week.

A contemporary pamphlet drew attention to the necessity of strict inspection by the Board to prevent corruption, when one relieving officer was paying as much as £80 a week to out-paupers. The Board set up a committee to examine carefully all bills and demands on the Union for sums greater than £1. A regulation was imposed that 'any workhouse officer receiving discount or accepting presents or allowing articles to be supplied which are not permitted is to be dismissed'.[12] Within the first few months of the Union the Clerk to the Board (interestingly enough, a former Walcot overseer) absconded with £800, the workhouse Matron was discovered to be a bootlegger (alcohol was forbidden to the paupers), and six 'corruptible' porters in the workhouse were dismissed. The importance

[10]*Second Annual Report of Board of Guardians.*
[11]*Guardians' Minutes, 1836*, p. 119.
[12]*Guardians' Minutes, 1836*, p. 56.

of these revelations is, not the slackness of the Board in allowing corruption, but their efficiency in exposing a sore which would have festered unseen under the old system.

But the most impressive part of the Board's work was with regard to lowering the amount of public spending, and all along it is obvious that the Guardians' sympathies lie more with the ratepayers than the paupers. Thus, when they swallowed their pride enough to send a deputation to their blood-foes, the city magistrates, it was to petition for poor persons to be let off the poor rates. The way they hoped to reduce their spending was to force as many people as possible to live in the workhouse—an environment ranging from the moderately unpleasant to the bestially inhumane—if they wanted to receive public assitance, rather than give them their dole in their own homes. 'Intelligent men in every country have recommended this method of relief in preference to a weekly pay out-of-doors, which is so evidently open to abuse and imposture'.[13] The parasites and malingerers imagined to abound would no longer apply for assistance. The figures illustrate their methods and bear out their expectations. In the parish of Hinton for example, so successful was this system, commonly known as the 'workhouse test' that the number of paupers (both in the workhouse and outside) dropped from one hundred before the institution of the Union to ten afterwards. Statistics of the annual expenditure of the Union[14] contrast favourably with the former average expenditure of the parishes now comprising the Union, calculated as £19,928.

	Annual expenditure	Paupers on in-relief	Paupers on out-relief
1837	£11,520	—	—
1838	£12,331	682	1704
1839	£13,703	691	1687
1840	£14,180	754	1765
1841	£14,525	749	1518
1842	£14,200	970	1648
1843	£13,865	1383	1794
1844	£13,470	1119	1816

[13]*The Working of the New Poor Law in the Bath Union,* by a Guardian.
[14]Bush: *Bath Union Notes.*

It will also be noticed that the number of paupers inside the workhouse goes up while the number receiving relief in their own homes remains fairly steady.

The greatest advantage of the larger administrative unit was its capacity to absorb large temporary increases in the amount of pauperism. As already mentioned, the lack of industry made these increases less likely to occur. Yet an overall survey of industry masks variations in different parishes. Those on the outskirts of the city were rapidly expanding, and Lyncombe for example had over five hundred textile workers, while St. Michael's parish in the centre of the city was stagnant in development and population. But though it had almost twice as many paupers as St. Michael, Lyncombe only paid slightly more than it, £2,018 as opposed to £1,869. Another comparison is still more startling. The parish of Twerton had three times the population of Hinton, and between six and seven times the number of paupers, yet only paid £320 to the Union as against £520 from the latter.[15] In this way, the burden of the rates could be shared and softened, albeit to the chagrin of the residents of St. Michael and Hinton.

All this is fine, and we may admit that the Guardians discharged their duty to those whose money they were spending both efficiently and honourably. But two open-mouthed dangers faced them. The first was that they might allow the paupers to live in the same. or worse, degradation, oppression and squalor as they undoubtedly had under the old system. They might do this out of simple neglect, or else out of a desire to make the workhouse so unattractive that on one would dare apply for poor relief—and the 'less eligibility' clause gave them an opening here. This policy the Board certainly did not openly show; their picture of workhouse life seems rather to have been idealistic, almost ridiculously Utopian:

> 'The worst punishment the Board can offer is comfortable maintenance in a well-regulated workhouse, in which he (the pauper) is kept clean, well-fed and well-clothed; is under a warm roof, and with abundance of companions; out of harm's way and far from that most prolific source of pauperism, the beer-house or gin-shop; and also in the way of receiving good from the regular ministrations of the Chaplain, and from the life of sobriety

[15]*Address of the Board of Guardians to the Poor Law Commission, 1837.*

and regularity which he is obliged to lead, until after a time he acquires a habit of order and decorum'.[16]

Whether they followed this policy secretly, only a study of work-house conditions can reveal.

The following delightful dialogue is in another contemporary pamphlet:

Straight Man: 'What did you think of the workhouse when you first entered it?'

Visiting Dignitary: 'I was astonished at the excellent food and good things provided for the inmates. I would not desire better provisions for my own family.'[17]

The standard workhouse dietary for the full week follows:

| | BREAKFAST | | DINNER | | | | | SUPPER | |
	Bread	Gruel	Cooked Meat	Potatoes or Other Veg.	Soup	Bread	Cheese	Bread	Cheese
	oz.	pints	oz.	oz.	pints	oz.	oz.	oz.	oz.
SAT. Men	8	1½	5 (Bacon)	12	—	—	—	6	1½
Women	6	1½	4	12	—	—	—	5	1½
SUN. Men	8	1½	—	—	—	7	2	6	1½
Women	6	1½	—	—	—	6	1½	5	1½
MON. Men	8	1½	—	—	—	7	2	6	1½
Women	6	1½	—	—	—	6	1½	5	1½
TUES. Men	8	1½	8	12	—	—	—	6	1½
Women	6	1½	6	12	—	—	—	5	1½
WEDS. Men	8	1½	—	—	—	7	2	6	1½
Women	6	1½	—	—	—	6	1½	5	1½
THURS. Men	8	1½	—	—	1½	6	—	6	1½
Women	6	1½	—	—	1½	5	—	5	1½
FRI. Men	8	1½	—	—	—	7	2	6	1½
Women	6	1½	—	—	—	6	1½	5	1½

Though neither mediaevally munificent nor excitingly varied, it is a healthy diet, and particularly so as the Governor of the Workhouse

[16]*The Working of the New Poor Law in the Bath Union,* by a Guardian.

[17]Spencer: *The Want of Fidelity in Ministers of Religion respecting the New Poor Law.*

had to eat the same as his charges. There were additional treats of tea and sugar for the aged, suet pudding, rice, treacle and milk for the children. An entry shown in the Minute Book concerning a complaint about mouldy bread shows that the Guardians were sufficiently concerned with the paupers' well-being at least to investigate the matter.

On the question of accommodation for the paupers the evidence is conflicting. One of the first decisions of the Guardians was to erect a new workhouse on Odd Down[18] to replace the several old ones, considerable trouble being taken over details of the structures and their continuing interest in the question is reflected by several entries in the Minute Book, for example, an order for better ventilation in the workhouse. Nonetheless, disturbing criticisms were made at the time, for instance, that there was no fire in the Sick Ward and that 'more than a hundred boys are sleeping four to a bed, and some men three to a bed.'[19] The total accommodation for 88 boys in 1840 was one schoolroom, one bedroom and one lavatory. The complete extent of the workhouse provided accommodation for 754 papers. With regard to sanitariness, the picture is more favourable. In 1843 out of 749 inmates, eighty-five died, and the report by Frederick Field, a surgeon, asserts 'there is nothing to warrant the idea of it [the workhouse] being other than a healthy place'. Little significance can be attached to the proudly quoted fact that the average age of death of paupers was fifty-four, as against a general average for Bath artisans and labourers of thirty-one-years, in view of the large number of aged paupers entering the workhouse; but it is more relevant that only 30 per cent. of the paupers died of epidemic and consumptive diseases, as opposed to 34 per cent. of the artisans and labourers.[20]

The arrangements for the employment of the paupers were less benevolent. Even the aged paupers, for whom the workhouse was to be regarded as an 'asylum' were set to picking oakum and sorting hair for upholsterers. Boys were taught field labour, shoemaking, tailoring and baking as well as 'all usual school instruction'. Able-bodied men were employed pounding rocks, quarrying, carrying coals, cleaning pigsties, scrubbing rooms and

[18]The workhouse buildings form part of St. Martin's Hospital.
[19]Spencer: *The Failure of the New Poor Law in the Bath Union.*
[20]De la Bèche: *Report on the City of Bath and its sanitary condition.*

bed-making among other activities.[21]   As to the clothing of the paupers there is little evidence. One interesting little saga does appear in the pages of the *Minute Book*, however. At various points in it there occur orders to the clerk to reprimand the clothing contractors, and eventually the contract was rather huffily terminated because certain articles of clothing did not come up to the sample provided. About a month later, there is an unobtrusive little entry in the book accepting these articles at a reduced cost.[22]

There are some more general points telling against the humanity of the Guardians. Visits to the paupers were allowed only once during the week, a stricter arrangement than for a debtors' prison even. Children were allowed out of the workhouse only occasionally under supervision. There was something of a scandal when the Guardians refused an offer for the children to see a Christmas pantomime one year. Men were separated from their wives in the workhouse but the Guardians defended themselves on the grounds that there was only one such case in the workhouse. And a charge was brought against the Governor of the Workhouse that he had confined a pregnant woman in the Refractory Ward for 24 hours without proper bedding and clothing, for which, being proved, he was 'censured'. All this evidence goes to draw a picture of the Guardians as honest and painstaking men, who without positively ill-treating the paupers, had a basic lack of sympathy for them; and we may acquit them of falling into the first danger.

The second great danger facing the Guardians was the temptation to shuttle everyone who applied for relief straight into the workhouse, which would have the effect of strongly discouraging such applications. In fact, it seems that many people were unaware that the Board relieved anyone outside the workhouse, though this is not the case. What the Board did do was to cut down ruthlessly the numbers to whom they were prepared to give out-relief, eliminating, as they thought, those who were trying to swindle the rate-payers, by offering them the workhouse or nothing. At the incorporation of the Union, 1,758 paupers (heads of families) were receiving out-relief to the tune of £10,311 a year. Twenty-five weeks later only 875 paupers were doing so at a cost of £5,360 a year.[23] Attention was drawn in a report from the Board to the Poor Law Commissioners

21Bush: *Bath Union Notes*
22*Guardians' Minutes, 1836,* p. 169.
23op. cit., p. 230.

to the fact that whereas £500 a year had been paid out to support 100 illegitimate children in Walcot alone, there were now no payments for bastards throughout the Union. Once the Board had started to give relief, it still demanded a certificate of health and circumstances of the pauper from his parish churchwarden every two months to continue it. About 15 per cent. of all out-relief was given in kind to stop, said the Guardians, the ratepayers' money being wasted on drink! They insisted on the principle that a pauper's primary dependence should be on his relatives. Thus there is an order in the *Minutes* that James Hutchin's son should be forced to maintain his father.

But the great question is whether by cutting down out-relief the Guardians were genuinely thwarting malingerers or else forcing into the workhouse people who by their rights under the Poor Law Amendment Act of 1834 or by the claims of common humanity, were entitled to relief 'out-of-doors'. To answer this a few individual cases will be examined. One example is an order in the Minute Book forcing an eighty-seven year old who asked for more out-relief into the workhouse.[24] A letter to a newspaper by the vice-chairman of the governors cites the case of two old women in the parish of Dunkerton one with cancer and one a cripple, who were ordered into the workhouse, the latter because she was illegally supplementing her relief by teaching nine children at twopence a week.

However, the cause célèbre of the new poor law in Bath was that of Ann Perry and Mary Price. This saga takes place in the following stages. Mary Price, a widow with four children, one of them earning eight pounds a year, was receiving 4s. 6d. weekly relief from her parish when the Union took over and reduced this to 1s. and two loaves. She was also supporting Ann Perry, an octogenarian of 'unexceptionable character', nominally as a servant, but who was bedridden for eight months of 1837, her last year. She therefore applied for relief on behalf of Perry, who was promptly ordered into the workhouse. Price then appealed to the magistrates, who in Bath as elsewhere had a more generous attitude towards pauperism than the Guardians, who ordered the Board to out-relieve Perry. Then, it was alleged, two Guardians visited Price and threatened to withdraw her own relief unless she withdrew Perry's application, which she did. Nevertheless, Price's relief was withdrawn, for as the Guardian's self-justificatory report remarks, she was earning 6s. 6d. a week at

[24]*Guardians' Minutes, 1836,* p. 178.

least from washing for a family, 'and in addition to this', they acutely observed, 'she has a valuable mangle, from which she just derived considerable emolument'. Unconvinced, the magistrates applied to the King's Bench (they had certain powers under Clause 27 of the 1834 Act), and the Guardians caved in. The episode of the Guardians' threats to Price may be discounted, but the attitude of the Guardians remains inexcusable and they seem throughout the ensuing publicity given to the case to have been more concerned with maintaining their authority against the magistrates than with righting a mistake or an injustice.

The death was reported in 1843 of Joseph West whose body 'was reduced by emaciation to a very skeleton'. He, his wife and four children received only 1s. and a quartern loaf every week. Their only food was dry bread and tea, twice a day. Reports of other deaths in the newspapers show that some had either been unjustifiably turned away by the Board or else were too afraid of the workhouse to apply at all. Thus in April 1837 three deaths were reported in the *Bath and Cheltenham Gazette*, of Diana Allen 'who died from neglect and starvation', of Benjamin Parry who 'died through the inclemency of the weather and the want of the common necessities of life', and of John Johnson, 'who for some time had no other lodging but a cowshed, died there alone'.

These examples are, of course, the most compromising for the Guardians that could be found; it would be both pointless and impossible to find instances where the individual decisions of the Guardians were sage and judicious, though no doubt many such exist. Nonetheless, these injustices, these fatal mistakes are mostly drawn from impartial and disinterested sources—they certainly did happen and if, as Acton says, 'the final judgement depends on the worst action', full account must be taken of them.

Printed evidence can only give a very pale and unfinished picture of contemporary controversy over the New Poor Law, diluted of the passion. The conflict in Bath was basically between the 'hard-line' Guardians and the only articulate and respectable opposition to them, the 'soft-line' magistrates. The mob did not enter as a third factor, and there were no riots such as those at Todmorden. The reasons for this are hazy, but both the function of Bath, as a sedate Spa resort, and its geographical position in phlegmatic Somerset, played their part. Except for the Price/Perry affair the Guardians made no notable blunders or provocations and one does not quite imagine them as the viciously mean Board in 'Oliver Twist'. Perhaps most important of all, Radical sentiment in Bath seems to have been channelled into the Chartist movement (see Chapter One). Thus attention and agitation was diverted from local government into wider political spheres.

The Guardians' bone of contention with the magistrates appears in the *Minutes:* '. . . that from the commencement of the Union in March, 1836 our endeavours have been greatly thwarted and partly paralyzed by the interference of certain magistrates'.[25] They protested that 'the feelings of the board are decidedly in favour of erring on the side of liberality'.[26] The magistrates on the other hand regarded the re-election of the Guardians as 'a thing most earnestly to be deprecated by everyone in whom a friendly feeling towards the deserving poor . . . has not altogether ceased to exist . . . Severity and disregard of the most sacred treasures of the human mind have marked the entire course of the administration entrusted to them.' If the Board had saved rates, they said, 'it is by introducing a degree of severity not intended by the law'.[27] Thus, if there was no rioting, there was considerable ill-feeling against the Guardians. There are references in the newspapers to accusations of bad bread in the workhouse, or that it was limited to two ounces a day. On a less credible level there were rumours that 'workhouse paupers are sold as slaves, thrown into the river, or into holes dug for them in the garden'. And in fact, hostile violence was not unknown. A porter of the workhouse was once directed to apply for a summons of assault against a pauper and an angry spectator after an incident at a pauper funeral.

People did suffer under the New Poor Law. The eight hundred odd who were refused out-relief were not all work-shy loafers, and it is one of the great virtues of modern democracy, to allow itself to be swindled, that the unfortunate may not go to the wall. The 1834 Amendment Act, by its virtual abolition of the Settlement Laws, genuinely made more work available, as agricultural labourers, for instance, could go without hindrance to the areas where they were needed. Some wounds were healed, as of neglect, maladministration, corruption. The greatest virtue of the Guardians as a freely elected

[25]*Guardians' Minutes, 1838–39*, p. 122.
[26]*The Working of the New Poor Law in the Bath Union*, by a Guardian.
[27]Barretté: *A Few Plain Facts*.

44

body was their lack of self-interest, and indeed their selflessness in giving up often valuable time for unpaid public service. They contrast happily with the pre-1834 Morpeth select vestry, a very liberal body, allowing paupers alcohol in abundance. Eleven out of its twenty members were brewers.

Though the work of the Bath Board was fairly rigidly defined by the Amendment Act, it was clearly not completely under the thumb of the central authority, and a great deal indeed depended on the quality of the men on the spot. Though there was no defiance of the Poor Law Commissioners as there was in some Northern Unions—there is no hint of dispute in the Guardians' voluminous correspondence with them—the Bath Board showed its individual qualities in its efficiency, determination to stamp out malpractice, and its concern that the workhouse inmates should live, if not in luxury, at least like men and not like animals. It also showed a reprehensible paranoia where its own actions were concerned, a violent reaction to hostile criticism, a refusal to admit its own mistakes. Throughout the Minute Books there is no record of a successful appeal against decision of the Board's whether on behalf of three orphans or dying octogenarians. The inimical attitude of the magistrates attempting, the Guardians thought, to usurp legal powers not theirs by right, was largely responsible for this. No special significance can be laid on the hostility of the magistrates to the Guardians, for this was a common phenomenon in the Southern Unions. Their efforts are seen in perspective when we consider that the problem of poverty in Bath was neither lacerating nor insoluble. The Guardians' task was made lighter and prestige higher by a general economic improvement in the 1840's.

Sources

Sources: (All in the Bath Reference Library, unless otherwise stated).
Minute Books of the Bath Guardians, 1836–39 (Bath City Record Office).
Poor House Committee Book, St. Peter and St. Paul, 1784–1812.
De la Bèche: *Report on the City of Bath and its sanitary condition, 1843.*
Sealed order of the Poor Law Commission establishing the Bath Union, 1836.
Second Annual Report of the Board of Guardians, 1838. ✕
First Quarterly Statement of the Board of Guardians, 1836.
Address of the Board of Guardians to the Poor Law Commission, 1837.
Receipt and Payment Book: St. Peter and St. Paul, 1836–39. ✕
Accounts, St. Peter and St. Paul, 1822–24.
Thomas Spencer: *The New Poor Law: Its Evils and their Remedies.*
Thomas Spencer: *The Failure of the New Poor Law in the Bath Union.*

Thom as Spencer: *The Want of Fidelity in Ministers of Religion respecting the New Poor Law.*

The Working of the New Poor Law in the Bath Union: by a Guardian.

Charles Barretté: *A Few Plain Facts, 1837.*

The Bath Journal.

Bath and Cheltenham Gazette, 1835–40.

R. S. Neale: *The Standard of Living, 1780–1844: a Regional Class Study* (in *The Economic History Review*, Vol. XIX).

John Bush: *Bath Union Notes, 1865.*

CHAPTER FOUR

Public Health and Housing in Bath

BRIAN WEIGHT

PROPERLY to estimate the health ... of the inhabitants of
Bath, it should be borne in mind that it is a place of much
resort for persons in affluent and easy conditions of life (among
whom females prevail), who reside in good houses, and for the
most part in well-ventilated streets, or crescents, and ranges of
building well exposed to the sun and winds, ...[1]

This comment on the matter in hand was made by a Royal
Commissioner responsible for an extremely detailed report to which
anyone interested in this period should certainly refer. But to see
the city merely as the pristine spa, as all fresh white Bath stone-work,
Georgian gems, and Perpendicular Abbey, is to view with eyes sadly
out of perspective. De la Bèche and his contemporaries could see the
other side of the coin equally clearly:

> In proportion as the Squares and Crescents filled with the
> affluent, the dens of Holloway filled with beggars. This was their
> camp, from whence they watched the visitors who were their prey,
> and eluded the corporation who were their natural enemies.

Bath did indeed have a second side. By 1830 we can no longer
think in terms of Georgian fashionable splendour, but of a sprawling
Spa which would very soon be opened to the inroads of industry by
the completion of the Great Western Railway's Paddington to
Bristol line in June, 1841 (see Chapter Six). No longer was there
a large transitory population. Bath had become a place of permanent residence for admirals, generals, civil servants, clergy, and

---

[1]De la Bèche: *Report on the State of Bristol and other Large Towns*, p. 25.

retired merchants, a dignified nucleus in sharp contrast to Beau Nash and his tribe of followers during the eighteenth century. Following closely behind this new influx came the poorer elements, searching for the stable employment which a large residential city can supply. By 1841, the population numbered 53,206 (including the outlying parishes).

There is to be found a very clear direct relationship between wealth and health, exemplified in the intermediate stage of the housing in which respective sections of the population found themselves situated. But before looking at these contrasting predicaments, let us deal with the general attitude of the Bath Corporation towards the upkeep of its famous city—'a place of universal resort'.

Perhaps the most striking impression received is one of disunity. No overall sanitary system existed. Walcot out-parish was under the jurisdiction of Commissioners who held authority by the Local Government Act of 1760—'An Act for paving, cleansing, lighting, watching and regulating the streets, lanes, ways and passages and public places'. Similar Acts existed for Bathwick, and the City district (the latter embracing the parishes of St. James, St. Michael, and the Abbey). Consequently, three separate bodies were operating. In both 1837 and 1840 the Town Clerk was prompted to action, calling a meeting of the Commissioners. On each occasion the meeting broke down through the obstinate possessiveness shown by the respective bodies towards their rights. The Town Clerk concluded: 'There are three local Acts which are conflicting and inadequate'. De la Bèche noted that, apart from Walcot, there was 'a total absence of public powers for drainage and sewerage, a singular state of things for so large a town'. A curious example of the ridiculous situation was the surfacing of York Street in the early 1830's, one side being paved, the other macadamised.

Nevertheless, all three city parishes did employ a force of scavengers who 'shall daily and every day before the Hour of Eleven in the Forenoon . . . sweep and collect together all the dirt, dust, filth, and rubbish'. These ancestors of the modern dustmen could be seen twice a week trudging the streets of Bath with their horse and cart, ringing a bell at every courtyard, passage or turning to give notice of their arrival. The refuse collected would then be taken off to a depot on the outskirts of the city and sold as manure.

Sewerage was dealt with in a more typically haphazard way, though with quite considerable success. No public powers existed

for drainage and sewerage, and consequently the removal of ex-
cretion from privies was not part of the scavenger's job. Luckily,
this was in any case only necessary when a blockage occurred in the
sewers. No person was permitted to bring a cart to empty any
'necessary, privy, or boghouse' before midnight or after 5.00 a.m.;
nor was this 'night soil' to be deposited in or near any of the city's
streets and public places. A breach of these regulations might
bring the offender several uncomfortable nights locked in the watch-
house, awaiting the statutory alternative punishment of a 10s. fine or
30 days hard labour![2]

Privies did not often need to be cleared in this way however,
since quite an extensive drainage system had been laid, cleansed by
water from the roofs. 'There are main sewers either in the streets or
in the areas of the houses, or behind the houses, with collateral or
branch drains from the houses into them.'[3] The whole system had its
effluence into the river with the exception of a few small cess-pits in
the suburbs. Only in the low-lying riverside areas—predominantly
of slum dwellings—were the sewers poor, constantly swollen and
blocked by flooding, and the houses often without a privy at all. In
comparison with other cities investigated by the Commisioners,
Bath was found to be well provided for despite the lack of administrative centrality.

A very similar situation existed as regards water supply. Springs
and natural wells were to be found in superfluity on the hills surrounding Bath. Those on Beechen Cliff, Beacon Hill and Bathwick
Down were all owned by the Corporation; but there were seven
other water companies, often in the hands of one of the great local
landowners—Sir Thomas Bloomfield's Company, Lord Manver's
Company etc.—each laying his own network of iron and lead pipes,
sometimes in competition, sometimes concentrating on his own
property. Only the houses of the very poor were without a supply,
the annual charge averaging at a very reasonable 27s. Of the 8,200
houses in the city, 3,000 were supplied by the Corporation who also
undertook to place six public conduits in the poor districts. A
certain Mr. Little, agent for the Circus Water Company, affirmed
proudly that the water in the pipes was unfiltered, being 'considered so
pure' as to render this precaution unnecessary![4]

[2]Act for Improving the City of Bath, 54 Geo. III (1814).
[3]*Report of Commissioners on Municipal Corporations, 1835.*
[4]*Report of Commissioners on Municipal Corporations, 1835.*

Not surprisingly, the general conclusion reached by the Royal Commissioners with regard to the sanitary measures taken in the city was that 'the streets are generally airy and good, the chief exceptions being in the lower and older part of the town'.

The 'lower and older part' of Bath had been shunned by the two John Woods when they built up what had been little more than a mediaeval walled town into an affluent resort between 1727 and 1776—and not without reason. Queen Square, Gay Street, the Circus, Brock Street, the Royal Crescent and the Assembly Rooms are all built on marls and limestones, high above the river water level and consequently dry or moist. Older streets like Southgate Street, Avon Street, Milk Street, Green Park Buildings and the lower part of Holloway are situated close to the river on alluvial flats mainly composed of clay. Hence the problem of flooding was ever present, as it has remained down to this day; and hence also the abandonment of this area by the great majority of citizens and their replacement by the poor and destitute. De la Bèche was singularly concerned over this situation:

> The floods are much felt in the tenements (nearly altogether occupied by the poorer classes) erected outside the city boundary, on that part of the alluvial flat of the Dolmead, where the discharge of the floods, from the bridges and encroachments on the river towards the quays, is much impeded. The houses in New-street, Dolmead, are so sunk in many places as to be beneath the water-level in high states of the Avon, and in floods they are inundated.

There can be little doubt that much of the flood problem was caused by encroachments on the river's edge, by the great numbers of bridges erected, and not least by the bulbous piers of the Old Bath bridge at the bottom of Southgate Street. In 1824, a Flood Relief Committee had been formed and had reported unanimously in favour of removing the obstructions; but the cost of £47,848 10s. 0d. proved too great, the committee was dissolved, and no action whatsoever was taken, temporary or otherwise. So the position worsened and any drains that were constructed in the river-side streets helped rather than hindered the inundation of germ laden flood water into the houses. Added to the dilapidated state of the houses disused because of their unsavoury site, we must also remember the way of life prevalent among new pauper inhabitants: 'Many are crowded and dirty. In the worst houses, twelve families,

50

frequently four persons in a room. The general state of the air (in the dwellings of the poorer classes) very impure'.

These statements by city councillor, Mr. Philip Duncan, bring us abruptly back to the relationship between wealth and health (see Appendix). With few possessions, the victims of industrial progress—farm hands no longer needed, Somerset textiles craftsmen unable to compete with Lancashire machinery—wandered to the prominent city to find employment and habitation, and were thrust into unwanted and insanitary buildings where a lack of moral values or hygienic standards very soon crept in. If no house or tenement was available on rent, the last resort was to go to one of the twenty-seven lodging houses to be found in the Holloway area.[5] The cost was 3d. per night and the possibility of sleeping two, three or four in one bed was high. It is little wonder that in Lyncombe and Widcombe parishes (including Holloway and where the population was largely of poor and the houses constantly flooded) the infant mortality rate was 1 in 2:

LYNCOMBE AND WIDCOMBE	1841 Population	Deaths	of which: under 5	of which: under 1
	9,920	163	72	50

These children died from convulsions, asphyxia, consumption, bowel complaints and chest inflammation. The disconcertingly short life of many of the poor stands in sharp contrast to the great age attained by the wealthy. Indeed, along with Bath's society reputation, it was its mild climate and respectable, well-built housing which attracted the well-to-do to retire into permanent residence in the city. The middle-aged and elderly wealthy far outnumbered the poorer elements, and the fact that three tenths of the 1,151 deaths in 1841 were of people over 60 years old bears out the statement by Mr. Field, a Lansdown Surgeon and registrar, who affirmed:

It has been often said, and I believe with truth, that the city of Bath contains a larger number of aged persons than any other place in the kingdom of equal size and population.

[5]i.e. The Workman's Rest.

At this time, Lansdown district extended to the banks of the river Avon, taking in the poorer areas of Avon Street and Milk Street. Consequently its high mortality ratio of 1 in 47·5 is not unexpected. Compare, '—a section of the part which lies low, and inhabited chiefly by poor people and vagrants . . . we find the ratio to be 1 in 40·3' with '—another section, of an elevated position, and inhabited almost entirely by the rich [the Crescent, Circus etc.] . . . the ratio there being 1 in 76'. Other areas with a large percentage of poor inhabitants were Walcot and, of course, Lyncombe and Widcombe; all having correspondingly high death-rates. In the Abbey and Bathwick districts we find mortality ratios of 1 in 51·3 and 1 in 61·4 respectively, these being the residential areas of the leading citizens and tradesmen.

Mr. Field's resumé of the health situation—'I cannot but conclude that Bath is a healthy place'—obviously needed the qualification—'On the other hand, we must take into account that a considerable amount of poor dwell in the city'. Field concluded his report by praising the medical facilities which Bath could provide for rich and poor alike.

> They [the poor] certainly exhibit great carelessness with regard to the preservation of the health of their children, and too often neglect to avail themselves of medical assistance until too late to be of service.
>
> There are many physical causes of disease in Bath. Witness the floods in the lower parts, their imperfect drainage, and the crowded and dirty state of the dwellings of the poor in various localities; and the disease there would be of great extent and fatal character were it not for the very active benevolence exercised towards the poor, and the great facility they have in obtaining medical aid from the hospitals and dispensaries with which the city abounds.[6]

Our view of the people's health would indeed be incomplete if we were not to investigate the 'medical assistance' available.

Bath had gained fame during the eighteenth century as a Spa whose hot mineral waters cured a great number of rheumatic complaints. Hence its most important hospital, the Mineral Water Hospital in Borough Walls, had been opened in 1742, centred on the

[6]De la Bèche, op cit., pp. 27–8.

medicinal use of the waters. A strange quirk in its foundation clauses barred residents of Bath from attending this hospital, but this peculiar state of affairs was rectified by an Act of 1830. By 1843, it had 86 beds for males and 47 for females, with an average number of patients at any one time of 120. Here, strict sanitary regulations were applied, the linen was well-aired, and in general the hospital was 'well drained and free from any unpleasant smell'. The establishment was, in fact, one of the best endowed and most luxurious in the country, and praise for its services were frequently forthcoming:

> It is a peculiar feature ... that no interest is required to gain admittance to its advantages—no recommendation of subscribers, governors, or any other person.[7]

Part of the hospital bathing amenities were set aside for out-patients—the poor being allowed their use completely free for medicinal purposes. Separate public mineral water baths also existed—the King's, Queen's, and Cross baths, the charge for use being 1s., 1s., and 6d. respectively. Little wonder that Mainwaring could proudly boast that 'the baths of this city are unparalled in any city in Europe'.[8]

Bath's second hospital was the Bath United Hospital situated in Beau Street and now occupied as the old building of the Technical College.[9] A smaller establishment, its average number of inmates was 65. This hospital had been founded 'for the reception of medical and surgical cases' and dealt with all the major diseases and illnesses not covered by the Mineral Water Hospital whose scope was naturally limited mainly to rheumatic and arthritic cases. It is not therefore surprising that in 1841 the Mineral Water Hospital had only three deaths, whilst the United had 56. Certainly, infections and fatal diseases could spread viciously in an age when medical science was still a novice in the field of life-saving cures: antiseptics and vaccination techniques were only at experimentation stage in the 1840's, and diseases like cholera and diarrhoea remained unchecked till the end of the century. A terrifying example was the arrival of 'cholera morbus' in Bath in the summer of 1832.

[7]John Earle, *Bath Ancient and Modern*, p. 267.
[8]R. Mainwaring: *Annals of Bath*, p. 320.
[9]In addition to the two hospitals mentioned, the city had two dispensaries for medicine—one at the end of Beau Street, the other at the end of Cleveland Bridge.

Since 1817, this disease had spread across two continents from its origin in Jessore, Bengal. Bills were rushed through Parliament to direct sanitary measures and to authorise the collection of a levy in towns, parishes or counties to cover the expense of combating the deadly threat. A Central Board of Health was set up in London and departments were formed in all the large towns. The disease hit Bristol in June 1832 and on 28th July the first case was reported on New Quay (now Broad Quay), the victim dying in a matter of days. A close watch was kept on all those who entered the city.

... Burial places were appointed, exclusively for cholera cases. Persons were stationed at the entrances of the city, to watch the ingress of travelling mendicants, and the receiving or mumping houses were continually under inspection. The benefits arising from a careful observation of these vagrants cannot be placed in a clearer point of view than by stating that, in Walcot alone, 539 vagrants were passed through that parish during the prevalence of the epidemic, without locating in the city.[10]

Despite this, by 28th August the disease had claimed nine fatalities. A timber shed on the Upper Bristol Road was turned into a hospital, as was a large warehouse in Avon Street. At length, the disease was checked, and by 17th October the Bath Board of Health pronounced the city to be free of its 'murderous hand'. 74 cases had been dealt with from which 49 deaths had ensued, over 70 per cent. of the fatalities being from among the poor whose living conditions (combined with some late summer flooding) provided an ideal breeding ground for the ravages of 'cholera morbus'.

One of the major constructional works of the corporation during the period under discussion gives explicit emphasis to the facilities open almost exclusively to that numerous section of the population, those 'in affluent and easy conditions of life'. This was the laying out of the Royal Victoria Park, opened in 1830.

The advantages which shady promenades and agreeable drives confer on any town or city, are too obvious to require ennumeration.[11]

The advantages, though 'obvious', were not open to all. The Park became a fashionable meeting place and none of the poorer

[10]R. Mainwaring: *Annals of Bath*, p. 403.
[11]R. Mainwaring: op. cit., p. 345.

elements of the city would show their faces there—especially since wardens had been appointed to 'eject' any uncleanly, undesirable personage. These wardens carried out their duties with the diligence of a police state, and another outlet for escape from squalor to a healthy atmosphere was closed to the ever-increasing numbers of poor.

As Bath filled with those who could afford the high prices asked for its beautiful houses, the tendency away from the social towards the residential produced many new erections which meandered over the approach slopes around the city, especially in the higher parts of Bathwick and Lansdown parishes. The detached villa, secluded within its own grounds, was in great demand amongst the more affluent citizens, a good example being the now-demolished St. George's Lodge in Oldfield Road. This neo-Georgian edifice built in 1841 was the home of a Bristol merchant named Collins, one of several business men who came to settle in Bath and began small commercial concerns, especially on the Lower Bristol Road. (Collins built a flour factory there in the early 1840's.)

Not surprisingly too, Bath was swept by the general nineteenth century frenzy of church building. In a fast-growing city the few churches which had sufficed in the eighteenth century (with the Abbey very much at the centre) were no longer enough. Hence the following list which shows the astonishing build-programme for a single decade:

St. Saviour's, Larkhall. Consecrated: 1829.
St. Mark's, Widcombe. Consecrated: 1830.
All Saint's, Weston. Consecrated: 1830.
Combe Down Church. Consecrated: 1832.
St. John's, Lower Weston. Consecrated: 1832.
St. Michael's, Broad Street. Consecrated: 1835.
St. Stephen's, Lansdown. Consecrated: 1840.
Catholic Apostolic Church, Henry Street. Consecrated: 1840.
Jewish Synagogue, Corn Street. 1841.

That these churches were well-endowed and well-supported by their respective parishes will be no more surpising.

But the poor continued to live in insanitary dwellings. In the 1830's humanitarians like the Poor Law champion, Edwin Chadwick, were mocked for their beliefs that material environment has a real effect on physical and mental well-being. The fashionable doctrine

55

of the time was 'laissez-faire'. The active benevolence exercised towards the poor, mentioned by Mr. Field in his report, remained their greatest salvation, combined with Bath's superb medical facilities which could stand favourable comparison with any other important provincial town in the country. Certainly, the poor of Bath were far better off than those in the Midland and Northern towns which were at the heart of our growing industrialisation. The atmosphere and sanitation of Bath's growing slum areas were purity itself when compared with the squalor which accompanied the hard labour of the Industrial Revolution.

This did not mean however, that vast improvements in health and housing standards were unnecessary in a luckier city like Bath. As we have seen, it too had difficult problems like many other cities—hence its choice as one of the fifty cities investigated by the Health of Towns Commission in 1842. De la Bèche was but one of many Commissioners who travelled around different parts of the country making detailed reports on the chaotic, disorganised and totally insufficient sanitary measures taken in England's major cities, a state of affairs which remained without any marked change during the 1830's.

Bath during these years provides a very clear picture of the gulf between the moneyed and the labouring classes, and until the basic conception (so eloquently broadcast by Edwin Chadwick and John Simon as successive General Medical Officers of Health in England) was accepted—that good accommodation breeds great advances in both the physical and the mental condition—the levelling process incorporating the far higher mean standard of health and housing that may be seen in modern English urban society would not be achieved. If we could have walked in the Bath of 1841, we would have agreed with the comment of Dr. Southwood Smith (giving his conclusion on his findings as a Royal Commissioner in London's East End): 'A clean, fresh, and well ordered house exercises over its inmates a moral, no less than a physical influence . . .'

Only with the acceptance of this assertion would the sharp juxtaposition of glory and grotesque become limited in this 'handsome town', and the realisation he brought home that good sanitation and housing are essential. The passing of the 1848 and 1867 Public Health Acts, the 1866 Sanitary Act, the 1867 Factory Act, and the 1872 Sale of Food and Drugs Act were all very much future events in the Bath of the period under discussion; but the tone of Southwood Smith's report is an important sign that the spirit of 'laissez-faire' was finally being displaced by a questioning of the relative human conditions. In 1845 only the future could tell whether any action would be taken to remove the incongruities beneath the surface appearance of Bath—'the beauty and variety of the scenery, the mildness of the climate, the excellence of the houses . . .' etc.

Not every scene was beautiful, nor by any stretch of the imagination was every house excellent. To investigate the truth of conditions in Bath 1830–41 is to penetrate the tissue-like skin of such superficial idealism which had found its first roots in 'the age of the Beau'.

Sources

De la Bèche: *Report on the state of Bristol and other Large Towns* (Bath Reference Library).

Report of Commissioners on Municipal Corporations, 1835. (British Museum, H.C. (1835) Vol. XXIV).

City Police Act, 54 Geo. III (British Museum, Local Acts (1814) c. cv.).

Report of Sanitary Commissioners, 1842 (British Museum, Lords (1842) Vol. XXVI).

R. Mainwaring: *The Annals of Bath, 1838.*

John Earle: *Bath, Ancient and Modern* (1864).

CHAPTER FIVE

Bath and its Entertainments

RICHARD SALTER

THE days of Beau Nash were gone and, though everybody knew it, nobody admitted it. The rôle of the town of 'Aquae Sulis' in Roman Britain had been unique; she was Britain's first 'spa'; her first entertainments centre; her first 'resort'. And as soon as the gentry of England again looked for entertainment to relieve their increasing boredom, as the eighteenth century began, Bath revived. Bath had less to offer to the violent and insecure days of the seventeenth century but to the new leisured society, Bath and her waters offered an unparalleled opportunity for entertainment.

Hence Beau Nash. Beau Nash symbolised the revival of Bath entertainments. When he arrived, they flourished; when he was gone, they declined. By the Age of Reform the decline was virtually complete.

The nature of the decay of Bath's social life was an intangible thing. It may hardly be noticed in newspapers and accounts of the 1830's which give the impression of an endless succession of brilliant concerts, balls, galas, processions, theatre successes, raree shows, soirées and all the rest. Yet the social 'scene' had indeed changed. Beau Nash's Bath was a city of the avant-garde. Young, rich, daring young men staked their fortunes on games of chance, their happiness on affairs of the heart and their lives on duels and challenges. The scandals and stories of the nation's nobility were fed from Bath. Within Bath itself gossip and pettiness of all forms were frowned upon. Bath's grand patrons, visiting the city to take the waters and sample her diversions, were above it all.

By the 1830's a complete change had come about. Dickens' Mr. Pickwick and Sam Weller found Bath a 'grass grown city of the

58

ancients'. What had been young, trend-setting, aristocratic, daring and extrovert had become middle-aged, middle-class, unoriginal, timid and inward-looking. Bath had led social evolution; now she feared it. 'Bath', it was said in 1832, 'was deserted by fashion, after having served as its Temple'.

The decline is indicated by the nature of the new building in Bath in the early 1800's. Except for the Victoria Park (begun in 1830), and the New Pump Room (completed in 1829), the energies of the local builders were directed to schemes wholly disconnected from the field of entertainments. On the one hand there was industrial and commercial building; the Kennet and Avon canal, the Great Western Railway, factories, bridges and workhouses, while on the other hand there was ecclesiastical building; four new churches between 1820 and 1832, and a 'face-lift' for the Abbey. Bath was fitting herself out for the commercial heyday and the Victorian Sunday.

These were the symptoms of decline. The reasons were many and varied. Among the most important was demand. Beau Nash's Bath offered something unique; the Bath of the Age of Reform did not. She faced competition from Leamington, Cheltenham and nearby Hotwells (Bristol), and from the new seaside resorts which were beginning to attract people from all stations of life, from George IV with his frequent visits to Brighton, to the common folk whose doctors were beginning to advise the efficacy of salt water in all cases of illness. The Romantic Poets had popularised the high moor, the rugged mountain and the silver lake; Bath could provide none of these.

A change in the sort of patron that Bath encouraged was a second cause of decline. Georgian Bath had attracted the rich, the noble and above all the young. Bath in the 1830's filled with the new middle-class, and chief among them the 'aspiring' middle-aged, hoping to advance the fortunes of their sons and daughters by adopting a strategic position in Bath. Not only were the new patrons poorer and less influencial, they were more numerous. Nash had met all comers personally and Bath's social community had been compact and whole. The increased numbers (Bath's population had increased tenfold between the early eighteenth century and the second quarter of the nineteenth century) meant a fragmentation. Cliques and groups evolved, preferring their own domestic entertainments to the public entertainments offered by the Master of Ceremonies.

59

Nor were Nash's spiritual descendants equal to this unfortunate development. James Heaviside (Master of Ceremonies 1818–35) and Colonel William Jervois (1835–44) were admirable citizens but nonentities in the field of entertainment.

Mention has already been made of the commercial developments felt even in Bath by the Age of Reform. The new rigours of the Industrial Revolution would alone have been enough to end the clamour for entertainments, but Bath's position was doubly unfortunate, since it was not even favourably placed in the new industrial society. The new centres were in the Midlands and the North. Bath, near Wiltshire's worn-out textile industry, was the centre of an industrial backwater.

Lastly, the decline of Bath's entertainment owes much to the improvements in communications. The opening of the Great Western Railway was hailed as the dawning of a new age for Bath, when new patrons would flow into the city on the fast, comfortable trains; yet the coming of the Railway and the general improvements in communications had in fact the effect of destroying Bath's social status finally. While travel was slow and uncertain every town in the country maintained its unique features. As travel became easier every town began to look the same. Bath was no longer special.

Now that it has been emphasised how much entertainments in Bath had changed by the 1830's, it is necessary to stress the ways in which things had not changed. Richard Graves had spoken of Georgian Bath in these terms;

> The greatest charity we can bestow on people of fashion at a public place is the furnishing them something new to talk of. A new singer, a new philosopher, a new rope-dancer, or a new preacher are objects equally amusing to the idle and indolent that frequent Bath.

The principle still applied in the Age of Reform. The traditional round of Concerts, Theatre and Balls, fêtes, processions, celebrations and races was spiced by the addition of as many novelties as men of ingenuity could contrive. All that was novel, gimmicky, weird or unnatural was a potential money-maker and conversation-piece.

'Traditional' novelities were always well received. Wombwell's menagerie visited Bath early in 1838, and Madame Tussaud in November 1831. A menagerie that visited Bath in 1832 advertised a 'Great Baboon, Howling Hyena etc., etc.' Among the planned features for the Victoria Park that were proposed in 1831 were a viaduct on the lines of the Regents Park tunnel, an aviary and a zoo. Perhaps enthusiasm for the latter project was dimmed when a Boa Constrictor escaped from a visiting menagerie at Bathwick in the same month! Luckily it drowned in the Avon.

Other curiosities fell into three categories; models and other artistic novelties, freaks and human novelties generally, and scientific novelties. The decade of the 1830's opened to find an exhibition in the Masonic Hall, York Street, of a 'splendid and extensive New Peristrephic PANORAMA OF THE LATE TREMENDOUS BATTLE OF NAVARIN'.[1] This was superseded by the end of the year by a similar 'Panorama of the conflicts in Paris', as the news of that year's disturbances began to reach this country. In October 1830 it was apparently a paying proposition to charge 1s. per head to see just one painting, Martin's '*The Fall of Nineveh*', and February 1832 found in Bath a 'microcosm of microscopic scenes'![2]

The human novelties drew the crowds ever more effectively; the discovery of an Albino Negro in America was accorded a considerable space in the *Bath Chronicle* in August 1832. In May of the same year Bath was entertained by an infant guitarist, Giulio Regondi, from Italy, and in January 1831 Michael Boal delivered a series of concerts of music which he made by tapping his chin! May 1830 was Bath's 'siamese' month. After a visit from 'the Siamese elephant . . . the *greatest* performer of the present day', Bath was graced by the visit of a pair of Siamese twins:

> . . . to give éclat to the entertainment (a Sydney Gardens breakfast), the extraordinary double Siamese youths were engaged to form part of the company and added greatly to the attractions provided . . . The number of gentlemen and ladies who attended the public breakfast was greater than usual . . .

The writer of this report in the *Bath Chronicle* has unconsciously made an important comment on his times. Physical peculiarities were as valid a source of delight to an audience as polished performances in singing or acting. Nor were the important advances in science being made at that time safe from the grasp of the novelty-monger. It can only be said that people of the day had insufficient

[1] *Bath Chronicle*, 18th May, 1830.
[2] *Bath Chronicle*, 14th February, 1832.

breadth of mind to see in scientific experiments any more than a source of novel entertainment. Among the advertised 'novelties' of 1830, for example, were a test of fire-proof asbestos, lectures in anatomy and a working model of a copper mine. In 1833 A. E. Binns advertised 'A SPLENDID COLLECTION OF EXOTIC INSECTS' in Silverthorne's *Bath Directory*.

Yet despite all these novelties which passed in the night the conventional sources of entertainment continued to attract the regular patronage of the wealthier citizens and visitors of Bath, for Bath was still a well-visited city with a recognised 'season' beginning in November and ending around the time of Easter. The first of these attractions was the Theatre.

Bath's Theatre, then as now, was the Theatre Royal.[3] This was not a time of Great Actors nor did any new Theatre pieces of note appear. *King Lear*'s tragic ending was still replaced by a 'tame' happy ending, and second-rate actors were lauded as though they were Garrick returned to life. The routine was for one actor of note to perform in a certain week, and to act the leading rôle in a large number of productions during that week. The performances which appealed to the Bath audiences of the 1830's seem comical in the extreme to us; among the offerings of 1830 were: *Harlequin Tom the Piper's Son*, *The Domestic Melo-Drama of Luke the Labourer*, *The Revenge* and *The Green-eyed Monster*.

Audiences might have come to demand a higher standard of performance if critics had been less mealy-mouthed for in this period the critics, traditionally forthright, sceptical and censorious, were exceptionally patronising, pleasant and kind to the plays they reviewed. One Mullery, acting Sir Toby Belch in *Twelfth Night*, in March 1833, 'went somewhat beyond the line of natural acting'. One dared not to say that he suffered from severe over-acting!

Next after the Theatre comes the endless succession of balls that gave Bath the outward appearance of a great fashionable resort. Some balls were public, as for example those given by the Master of Ceremonies. Others were thrown by clubs and societies, while others again were occasional, thrown to celebrate or to inaugurate. The ball was a convenient standard form of entertainment—once food and music were provided no other arrangements were needed—those who attended provided the entertainment by furnishing talking

---

[3]The original building in Orchard Street was closed in 1805. It was managed by John Palmer, the originator of the mail coach system.

points for each other. The ball was supremely social. One attended in order to be seen (with important people or with a new dress) or to see others. This was the very element for those ambitious middle-aged parents already described as the backbone of Bath's social structure.

The York Club threw an annual ball; so did the Master of Ceremonies. There was an annual Ball on 'Twelfth Night', and between 1830 and 1832 Balls were held to finance the new Victoria Park. Sometimes fancy dress was the order of the day—patrons of the 'Twelfth Night Ball' of 1832 wore costumes of the time of Henry VIII. Another famous king was fêted on 30th January in the same year, for a ball was thrown to commemorate the anniversary of the 'Martyrdom of King Charles'.

The appendix includes a contemporary account of a typical Ball of the period—the pedantic style and the forced delight are particularly the products of the age.

Music has always played a significant part in any account of entertainments. Of course Bath's patrons were well versed in music and were used to the 'incidental music', always provided at balls, fêtes, processions and indeed on almost all important occasions. But music was also an important source of entertainment in its own right. In January 1830 Bath welcomed the Rainer Minstrels from the Tyrol, while Paganini visited Bath in 1832, and intense anti-Russian feelings during the Polish uprisings of 1830-31 did not dull the enthusiastic welcome given to the visiting Russian Horn Band in December 1831. Enthusiasm for music led to the founding of a Royal Harmonic Society in Bath in 1832. During the summer of 1832, two Promenade concerts were given each week in Sydney Gardens, but not all of Bath's musical efforts were open to all. This was the time of the 'soirée' where the musically inclined members of social circles performed their party-pieces. This tendency for social 'rounds' to evolve has already been suggested as one of the reasons for Bath's decline as an entertainments centre. Culturally self-sufficient cliques were unwilling to subscribe to a system of public entertainments, and that system could not survive without their patronage.

Eating and drinking were the bases of many forms of entertainments at this time as at any other. Clubs gave dinners just as they threw balls—the Conservative Dinner was a great event in the annual calendar, as was the dinner for Officers of the North Somerset

63

Yeomanry—at least for those who were eligible. But the poor did not go without a measure of revelry. The increase in the number of cider shops was a growing worry to upright citizens, and to combat it a Temperance Society was established in February 1832. It was not hard for the authorities to equate drunkenness among the poor with 'radical' subversion. A People's Rights meeting in 1838 was condemned by the *Bath Chronicle* as a 'Blackguard Assemblage', a mere excuse for a drinking bout. (See Chapter One.)

Food provided the only entertainment for some of Bath's poor souls. Christmas was the time when charitable individuals and institutions made gifts—of food, of drink and sometimes of an evening's entertainment, to the inmates of the city's institutions—prisons, work houses and orphanages. On the whole it is difficult to obtain any picture of the way in which Bath's poor entertained themselves at this stage. This was the age in which Factory Reform was resisted by many for fear that the poor might acquire 'vicious habits' through having too much leisure time. In all probabilities the poor of the city kept themselves to themselves in their humble homes during their few leisure hours. On special occasions they swelled the number at processions and open-air meetings, only to fade back into the drab routine of their dawn to dusk work.

Events, past, present or future, were frequently celebrated with food and drink, as is shown by a series of Reform dinners begun in 1831 to support the movement for Parliamentary Reform. In February 1832, the Scots of Bath celebrated the Anniversary of Burns in the manner of their kind at the Caledonian Tavern.

Nor was gambling entirely absent from the bill of fare offered by Bath to its patrons. The Bath Races were held biennially in the Spring and Summer and were always the occasion for a week of fêtes, balls and carnivals. Card-playing assemblies also flourished during the season though those days were gone when gentlemen lost their fortunes in a night's game.

Fêtes offered a very varied diet of entertainment; some music, some of the 'novelties' viewed earlier, some food and some drink. A Sydney Gardens fête of 1835 provided 'A Gigantic Crown, a Pantomime Group, an Immense Balloon, the two escanoteurs', and many other entertainments eagerly enjoyed by the people of the time.

This completes the menu of entertainments which Bath offered. In addition, the cultured Bathonian could dabble in literature, or take advantage of a new interest in art, as shown by the foundation of a series of art exhibitions. Or he could cultivate his garden, helped by the newly-founded Floral and Horticultural Society (1834).

And what did the Bathonians of the Age of Reform have to celebrate? They had much indeed. It was a decade of political, social and royal events that provided endless opportunities for celebrations. In January 1831, William IV acceded to the throne, accompanied in Bath as elsewhere by gay galas, carnivals and processions. His Coronation in September was celebrated with Church services, parades, illuminations, galas and fêtes. The Coronation festivities of 1838 honouring the new young Queen Victoria were less successful in Bath. Bitter feuds between Tories, Whigs and radicals, embracing questions of finance, the importance and even the necessity of having a monarch, brought many committee meetings to an untimely end. Nonetheless the Coronation was loudly heralded in Bath with bells, cannon, flag-waving, processions, charitable dinners for the institutions, more fêtes, balls and the gayest expressions of loyalty witnessed for some time.

To close the decade came the Queen's marriage in 1840 and the birth of Edward, Prince of Wales, in 1841, both further subjects for celebration. Ironically there were celebrations too of the events that were to do most to complete Bath's decline. The 1832 Reform Bill, symbol of the Age of Reform, was celebrated by the erection of a Reform Column, and the opening of the Great Western Railway along its whole length in 1840 was another cue for celebration. Perhaps, though, this abundance of celebrations itself speaks of Bath's decline—the spirit of Bath's entertainments was no longer spontaneous—it needed an excuse, an occasion, to bring forth displays of gaiety.

We can hardly criticise the Bathonians of the Age of Reform for failing to recognise that their city no longer offered what it had offered before. Every city at any time believes in the excellence of what it has to offer. But it is strange to detect in Bath during this period two voices—the one asserting the successes of the present, the other lamenting the loss of past glories. Within one month (January 1832), the *Bath Chronicle* was able on the one hand to predict confidently a splendid season:

> We have every reason to believe that the present season will be one of the gayest which Bath has witnessed for some time past.

And on the other to report the Master of Ceremonies, vainly trying to encourage new patronage to 'this once-favoured city'.

Similarly while the Bath Races were cut back from three to two days in 1833, the Assembly Rooms were closed during no week between October 1835 and October 1836. Sometimes Bath recognised the pressures of a newer, faster age on her leisure pursuits. The *Bath Chronicle* commented on the widespread rural disturbances of 1830:

> We fear ... that the present outrages will have a bad effect on the Bath season, inasmuch as many families will refrain from leaving their houses in the country, lest they should be attacked and pillaged in their absence.

At other times the obvious failure of some entertainment was dismissed with as much politeness as the commentator could muster. At a Sydney Gardens Gala of 1838, 'the attendance was not commensurate with the exertions of the proprietor'.

Bath's social decline seems real, yet the continued success of her entertainments seems real too. Which was genuine and which was illusory? Was there still substance in Bath's entertainments despite the appearance of decline, or was Bath dead behind a facade of gaiety?

Sources

Bath Chronicle.
The Bath Journal.
Silverthorne: *The Bath Directory, 1837.*
The National Commercial Directory.
L. Melville: *Bath under Beau Nash and After* (1926).
Spender and Thompson: *The Story of the English Towns—Bath* (1922).
D. J. Jeremy: *The Social Decline of Bath* (in *History Today*, April 1967).

CHAPTER SIX

Bath and its Communications

MARTIN HEMMINGS

'THE CALAMITY OF RAILWAYS'

MR. BRUNEL, in his plan for reducing the population of your gay City by taking a short trip to London, wants to drag them at intervals on their journey through no less than nine tunnels, the first of which is under the high land near Box, which will be nearly two miles in length and on an inclined plane . . . Does not this tunnel alone present an obstacle to the conveyance of passengers quite impossible?[1]

INTRODUCTION

With new dimensions, ever more complex and fascinating, being opened up for present-day travellers, we are on the threshold of what may eventually turn out to be a transport revolution of unparalleled proportions. Today's generation, therefore, should be well equipped to appreciate and sympathize with the fears and doubts for the unknown which revealed themselves among the passionately superstitious and highly religious society in Bath in the 1830's, as the Great Western Railway became something more than a pencilled line across the map of England.

There were those whose foresight and vision outweighed their scepticism. But, as might be expected, the majority shared the apprehensions and misgivings of Ruskin, when he stated that: 'Railway travel is not travelling at all; it is merely being sent to a place, and very little different from becoming a parcel'. Macadam, whose life had been so intricately bound up with the development

[1]Letter to the *Bath Chronicle*, May 1835.

of road transport, referred to the 'Calamity of Railways'—they certainly sounded the death-knell of the Turnpike Road wherever they had been constructed. A new complexion had been given to transport and communications, and Bath after 1841 had to undergo the difficult process of adaptation. Bath had been linked to places that none but the very rich or very fortunate in the city had actually visited. Not that everyone could afford to travel by railway—far from it. But news was spread more quickly, the mail service (when it was eventually universally delivered by rail) was subject to less delays, and important goods could be conveyed in and out of the city with greater ease. A gentle revolution had been enacted in Bath, as in all the towns and cities along the length of the railway—not a political, industrial or agricultural revolution as such, but with a significant impact on each of these spheres of life.

PRE-RAILWAY TRAVEL

(i) 'It is good to be out on the road, and going one knows not where'—*Tewkesbury Road*.

The system of main roads in Bath was the responsibility of the Bath Turnpike Trust, established in 1707 as the first of its kind in North Somerset. This Act, available for public perusal in Bath Reference Library, set up the Trust to maintain a network of seven roads radiating from the city and, in order to defray the cost of maintenance, to collect tolls from those who used them. The steady increase in road traffic at that time necessitated a considerable improvement in both the surface and width of many of the local highways. To accommodate the coaches, waggons and carriages, which were passing ever more frequently, the J.P.'s (who were responsible for the appointment of Trustees) were empowered to widen their roads up to 20 feet, so long as no houses or gardens were damaged. The compensating tolls charged varied from 1d. for every horse, upwards to 1s. for four-wheeled carts and stage-coaches, hackney-coaches and waggons drawn by more than four horses.

Despite financial problems for part of the eighteenth century (£2,400 of the £3,000 originally borrowed in 1707 remained unpaid and creditors were suing for their money), the Bath Trust had grown both in physical size and financial stature since its conception. By 1820, its yearly income was £11,870, it administered and maintained some 51 miles of road, collected tolls (farmed out by the Trust to individual Toll-gate keepers), from 51 gates[2] and had five weighbridges within the City of Bath alone. The boundaries of the Trust had been substantially extended, so much so that, for administrative purposes, the roads were grouped into three sub-districts. The first group incorporated the London Road (starting east of Lambridge), the Colerne Road and the Lansdown, Wick and Abson Roads (starting east of Lansdown Place). The second grouping comprised the Upper Wells Road, starting south of Bath Bridge; the Warminster and Frome Roads, starting from Devonshire Buildings via Entry Hill; the Combe Hill Road; and the Combe Down and Claverton Roads, starting at the top of Entry Hill over Combe Down to join the Bath–Bradford road at Limpley Stoke. Lastly, there was the third zone—the Lower Bristol and Lower Wells Roads, starting at Old Bridge; and the Upper Bristol Road from the western boundary of the city, with a link to the Lower Bristol Road via the Newton Bridge.

The other roads within the city were under the direct auspices of the respective parishes until 1835, the Trust's powers of paving, lighting, cleansing and maintaining certain city streets having been repealed in 1757.

Profitable certainly, but how safe were the roads around Bath? The newspapers of the 1830's recounted many disturbing instances of petty highway robberies:

> About half-past 8 o'clock on Wednesday evening week, as Mr. Granger, a respectable farmer of Corsham, was returning home from this city, when near the cross-roads at Bathford, he was attacked by six men, who pulled him from his horse, threw him into a ditch by the roadside and proceeded to rifle his pockets. The exertions of the villains to prevent Mr. G. from making any alarm were so violent that he was at one time nearly strangled; and it was only by giving them the whole of the cash he had with him which fortunately was only two sovereigns, that his life was spared. The men wore smock frocks, and after the robbery ran towards Bath.

[2]The main Toll-gates or Turnpikes within the area of the city were situated at Grosvenor Place, Lansdown Road (near St. Stephen's Church), the top of Wellsway (the Burnt House Turnpike), the Lower Bristol Road, Claverton Street, the New Warminster Road, Newton Bridge, Widcombe Hill (bottom), and Combe Down (at the top of Foxhill Lane (see also Appendix G).

Another incident is noted in Bell's *Life in London*, (8th April, 1832):

At the Taunton assizes, three men were found guilty of breaking into the dwelling-house of Evans Taylor, who kept the Turnpike-gate at Bathford, and robbing him of £13 and his watch. Sentence of death recorded.

These were scarcely incidents to make Dick Turpin look to his laurels, but were nevertheless enough of a warning to add to the clamour in the city for a regular police force. Such matters were discussed at the monthly general meetings of the Trust (held in the Guildhall), but the Trustees showed reluctance to patrol their roads. Their money, they felt, could be spent in better ways. For instance, the Avon still provided a natural barrier to efficient road communications. (There was only the Old Bath Bridge and, to the west, the Newton Bridge.) On 16th April, 1835, an advertisement appeared in the *Bath Chronicle* inviting stone-masons and others in the building trade to tender for work on a new iron and stone bridge across the Avon. On 6th May, a well-attended meeting was held at Hetling House, when 'the plan for a bridge with a cast iron arch was unanimously adopted'.[3] Prospective shareholders were to pay £5 per share, with eight days allowed for payment. The foundation stone was laid on 23rd July, 1835, and the bridge opened by Lord James O'Bryan on 10th November, 1836. The North Parade Bridge, as it came to be known, provided a vital new crossing-point of the river and significantly assisted the flow of traffic, especially that of market traders from the fertile Avon Valley, at the same time easing the load on the Old Bridge.[4]

Improvements were simultaneously being made to the approach roads to Bath. In May 1832, a new wider road was opened to link the city with the Newton Bridge—a stretch of road now well-known as Newbridge Road. Moreover, the neighbouring Black Dog Turnpike Trust (of Frome and Warminster) planned in 1833, and constructed a new[5] road to follow the Avon valley from Limpley Stoke to Bath, thus by-passing the arduous ascent over Brass-knocker, Claverton Down to Holloway. Bath became more easily accessible to heavier vehicles, especially in winter, benefiting by a speedier delivery of both produce and mail from the south and west.

[3] *Bath Chronicle*, 7th May, 1835.
[4] Tolls were collected from the toll boxes still visible on the Bridge.
[5] i.e. the New Warminster Road.

The mail, in fact, was a subject of considerable controversy. Although the *Bath Chronicle* of 26th January, 1832 noted that a re-routing of the London-Bristol mail via Marshfield and Chippenham had meant an earlier delivery in Bath by some thirty minutes, a letter of 18th July, 1836 to *The Bath Journal* put into words the thoughts of many Bath citizens:

> Mr. Editor . . . letters and papers are detained from six o'clock . . . until nine; but . . . in many parts of the town, the detention is even for a much longer period than three hours. This loudly calls for amendment . . . I would observe that the Post Office is situated at so great a distance from many quarters of the city, that the inhabitants have a right to look for the establishment of regularly authorised Receiving Houses (as in London) at every half-mile or thereabouts; the Postman's bell is little to be depended on if a pelting storm makes it expedient for him to circumscribe his route, for in such cases I have been obliged to send my servants after him, to the said servant's discomfort, and the payment of the penny besides.

Such delays cannot be blamed so much on the state of the roads as on the inefficiency and lack of coherent organisation of the postal services. The implementation of the universal 'penny post' in 1840 did much to rectify the confused pattern of complicated letter charges and uncertain deliveries. Such was the public ignorance about postal rates in 1839 indeed that the *Bath Chronicle* felt obliged to publish an article of intended clarification:

1. No general post letters to be charged more than 4d., provided they do not weigh more than half an ounce; 8d. if less than one ounce; and an additional 8d. for every fraction exceeding each ounce.

2. No advantage will accrue from pre-payment of letters not chargeable more than two postages, as double postages are to be levied upon the receivers only upon letters exceeding one ounce in weight, when not pre-paid.[6]

But certain sections of the population were still displeased. A Bath Association for the Due Observance of the Lord's Day was established under the Rector of Bath, the Reverend W. J. Brodrick. They pursued a campaign of opposition to the delivery of mails and

[6]*Bath Chronicle*, 5th December, 1839.

to the operation of trains on Sundays. The controversy was brought to the fore in 1841 by a series of correspondence in the *Bath Chronicle*. The many Bathonians with deeply-held religious convictions were genuinely shocked by the use of the Sunday, but among their ranks came fanatical reactionaries whose hatred of the railway was such that to stop its running on one day in seven was, to them, a victory of considerable magnitude.

(ii) The Kennet and Avon Canal was a costly addition to the local landscape. It took some 15 years of labour and £900,000 to complete and was not opened for its whole length until late 1810. Only a quarter of a century later, however, before it had had an opportunity to show the full profits expected of it, its future prosperity hung in the balance. The railway era had dawned, casting ominous shadows for all those with vested interests in the Canal. Nevertheless, these were the years of maximum success, with annual receipts over £40,000 between 1830 and 1840 and a dividend for shareholders averaging just over three per cent.

In the months of March and April 1830 alone, 9,415 tons of goods were carried on the Canal. The comparable tonnage for the River Avon was just 1,655. Not that the Avon was a serious competitor to the Canal. Frequent weirs, difficult undercurrents and vulnerability of flooding were considerable handicaps to Avon transportation. By Canal, on the other hand, despite the extensive lock systems in Bath and Devizes, goods could be shipped from Bristol to London in just four days. But canals thought in terms of days, railways in hours—clearly it was not surprising to find the Kennet and Avon Canal Company in the forefront of opposition to the Great Western Railways Bills in 1834 and 1835. But such resistance, spirited as it was, was in vain, and the Act was passed in the summer of 1835.

The sun did not shine that summer for the Canal Company. They had to act fast. In 1837, it was decided to allow traffic by night as well as day, and by 1841, fly-boats up to 15 tons were permitted on the Bath–Reading section of the Canal. But representatives of the Company, sent to investigate the effects of the new London and Birmingham Railway on the trade of the Grand Junction Canal, had returned with disturbing reports. By 1839, the Company was buying its own shares as soon as these became available. But even so, resources were dwindling appreciably—not even the £7,000 paid by the Railway Company as compensation for having to re-route the

Canal while the line through Sydney Gardens was being constructed, helped the situation. (It even took almost a year to get this money, as the G.W.R. Company felt the £20 per hour damages claimed by the Canal Company were grossly excessive.)[7]

The opening of the G.W.R. line for its whole length in 1841 marked the effective end of the Canal as a means of communication. Local trade was not severely affected at first—coal was still brought in its usual quantities from the Camerton area via the Somerset Coal Canal and the Kennet and Avon. But the more profitable Bristol–London trade, on which the ultimate economic future of the Canal depended, was dealt a blow from which it never recovered. Receipts crashed, from over £51,000 in 1840–41 to less than £40,000 in just one year. Slight economies were made in both wages and manpower in 1841—but this was an entirely fruitless attempt to effect a recovery. Only a sentimental businessman could be expected to send his goods on the slower Canal journey from Bath to London. And there were as many of this breed then as there are today!

THE COMING OF THE G.W.R.

'Railway termini . . . are our gates to the glorious and the unknown'—Forster: *Howard's End*.

Although both road and canal transport were proving themselves adequately profitable in the 1820's and early 1830's, the first successful experiments with railway travel in the North of England (particularly the Liverpool and Manchester Railway) influenced some far-sighted West Country minds. Suggestions were put forward for the building of a railway in this part of the country, notably the 'Bristol and London' Railway Scheme of May 1832, but the reluctance of businessmen to convert their enthusiasm into currency prevented any real progress. The planners were not disheartened. Their diligence was rewarded, eventually, by a successful public meeting in Bristol on 30th July, 1833 'to take into consideration the expediency of promoting the formation of a rail road from Bristol to London'. The delegates—from the Corporations of Bristol, the Bristol and Gloucestershire Railway, the Bristol Chamber of Commerce, the Bristol Dock Company and the Society of Merchant Venturers—decided that a company should be launched and that the machinery for obtaining parliamentary powers should be put in

[7]*See* Clew: *The Kennet and Avon Canal*, pp. 88–95.

motion. Isambard Kingdom Brunel, then only 27, was engaged as engineer. Of the two short-listed routes—one along the Vale of Pewsey, then following the Kennet valley; the other, as surveyed by George Hennet, through Swindon and North Berkshire—Brunel chose the latter, the cost of construction, he estimated, being slightly over £2,800,000. At his suggestion also, the title 'Great Western Railway' was adopted in August 1833.

The first Bill—to build the two end sections of the line between Bristol and Bath, and Reading and London—was introduced into the Commons in March 1834. The promoters encountered vehement opposition from rival industries, including the Kennet and Avon Canal, but they cited the delays on the canal due to frost, drought and flood as valid reasons for rapid development. The Bill, however, was thrown out by the Lords, by a majority of 17, where it was considered neither 'Great' nor 'Western'. Strategy was now changed —and in 1835, a second Bill, this time for the complete line, was put forward. With the Boxhill Tunnel included in this scheme, violent objections were put forward:

> Consider the confined unwholesome air of the tunnel, which would be ventilated by no upright shaft, and the temperature would be that of a well!! Also the danger; the positive imminent risk of life—to say nothing of the minor evils of utter darkness and concentrated noise!![8]

Such sentiments are ridiculous to us today, but were perfectly plausible and understandable then—to the extent of being fostered in the Press. Nevertheless the Bill duly received the Royal Assent in August 1835. The G.W.R. Company was made into a corporation and allowed to raise capital to the extent of £2,500,000. A good deal of land had to be purchased in the city of Bath, and certain restrictions were imposed on the Company. For instance:

> The Company is not authorized to drain, divert or otherwise intermeddle with any Springs, Streams, Watercourses, Mains, Pipes, Reservoirs, or Cisterns of Water in the Parishes of Lyncombe, Widcombe or Bathwick in the county of Somerset.

No part of the Railway was to cross a turnpike road on the level, and the Act was specific on the matter of tunnels under such roads:
> ... and when such tunnel (under the Lower Bristol Turnpike

[8]Letter to *Bath Chronicle*, May, 1835.

74

Fig. 9   A view of the new toll-house on the London Road near Bailbrook

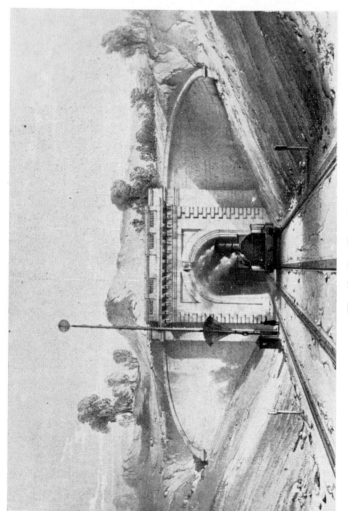

Fig. 10   Box Tunnel

Fig. 11   A view of Bathwick Bridge

BEWARE!!

ELECTORS SWORN IN AS

SPECIAL CONSTABLES

RECEIVING MONEY

LOSE THEIR VOTES.

No ELECTOR can be COMPELLED to serve as a SPECIAL CONSTABLE.

BATH : December 1, 1852.   [G. WOOD, PRINTER.]

Fig. 12   A warning to electors

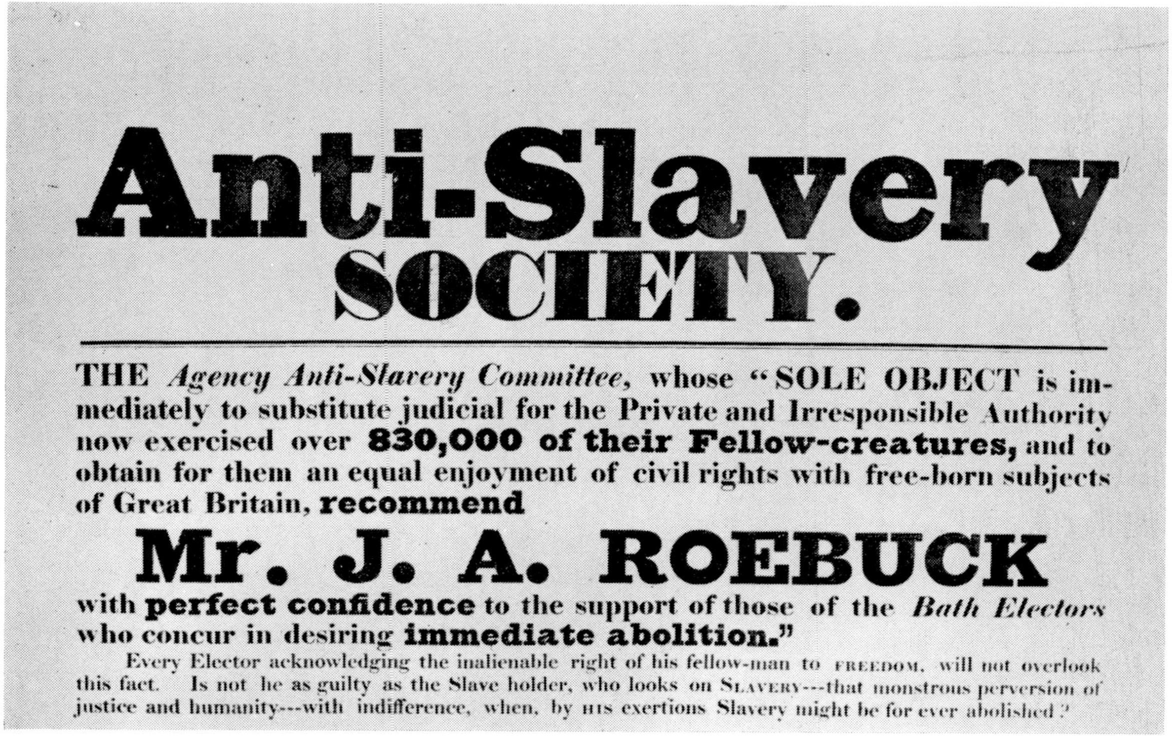

Anti-Slavery SOCIETY.

THE *Agency Anti-Slavery Committee*, whose "SOLE OBJECT is immediately to substitute judicial for the Private and Irresponsible Authority now exercised over **830,000 of their Fellow-creatures**, and to obtain for them an equal enjoyment of civil rights with free-born subjects of Great Britain, **recommend**

Mr. J. A. ROEBUCK

with **perfect confidence** to the support of those of the *Bath Electors* who concur in desiring **immediate abolition.**"

Every Elector acknowledging the inalienable right of his fellow-man to FREEDOM, will not overlook this fact. Is not he as guilty as the Slave holder, who looks on SLAVERY—that monstrous perversion of justice and humanity—with indifference, when, by his exertions Slavery might be for ever abolished?

Fig. 13   Anti-Slavery Society in support of Mr. Roebuck

Proclamation

Whereas,
SEVERAL
Silly Animals
Have within the last day or two
Hired LION SKINS
FROM THE MENAGERIE OF
Mr. H. VAN HOBSON-HOUSEN,

For the avowed purpose of *endeavouring* to frighten the honest part of the community; Persons are requested not to be alarmed at these foolish Animals. On close inspection it will be found that the long Ears are still too prominent to be concealed, and although they do their best to *roar most majestically,* yet the Kickerapoo Bray is evidently uppermost.

Printed by S. GIBBS, Union Passage, Bath.

Fig. 14   Derision aimed by Mr. Roebuck at his rival Mr. Hobhouse

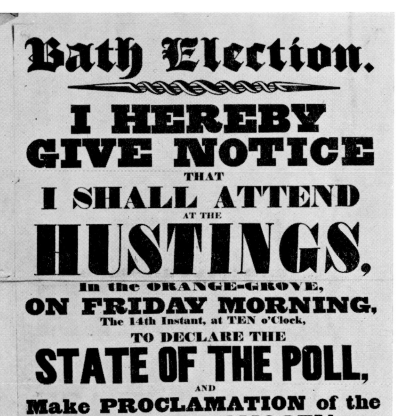

Fig. 15   Notice to declare the state of the poll

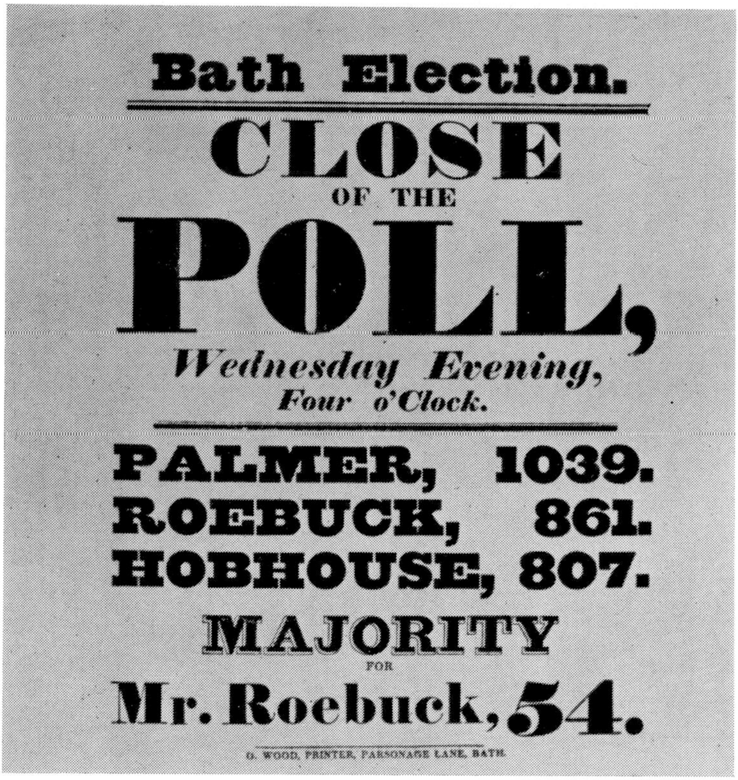

Fig. 16   The election results

Road) is completed, there shall be, if required by the said Trustees of the Bath roads, one foot and six inches clear between the top of the Masonry of such tunnel and the surface of the said road.[9]

The political talking to one side, the legal battles for purchase of land at last overcome, the moment for actual construction had arrived. The various portions of the line were contracted out, and the navvies, many recruited 'from the North' and from Ireland, but many also of local parentage, were set to work. Thomas Gale, the Officer Porter at Bath G.W.R. Station from 1852, writing of the building of the line, echoed the thoughts of middle-class Bath society to the influx of these workers—'Drunkenness and fighting were carried on to an alarming extent; no teetotalism was known . . . with that class of men.' Such an attitude was understandable, if not predictable, but could not detract from the absolutely vital nature of the navvies' work, however inebriated, in an age before large-scale mechanical aids to construction.

The work on the line presented few extraordinary problems— except for the construction of Boxhill tunnel. This is really a story in itself. The first trial shaft through the oolite and limestone hill was begun in February 1836 and took almost a whole year, before the original contractor, Horton, commenced sinking the actual 300 feet working shafts, ventilation holes and light access holes for the tunnel. Before these initial stages had all been completed, however, Horton failed his contract and this part of the work had to be finished by the Company themselves. The contract for the tunnel was then tendered out to Mr. George Burge, of Herne Bay, whom Thomas Gale calls 'a very rich and able man of business', and who, at that time, was engaged on the St. Catherine Docks scheme in London.

By the terms of his contract, Mr. Burge had to work the tunnel by manual and horse power, and only one 60 horse-power steam engine was permitted to pump water out of the shafts. But water, always a menace under the porous rock, rose to 56 foot in one shaft in November 1837 and flooded the tunnel. Consequently, work was ceased until July 1838, after another 50 horse-power steam engine had been allowed in to operate an extra cleaning pump.

The Corsham end of the tunnel had been sub-contracted to Messrs. Stothert & Lewis of Bath, but owing to the flooding of 1837, they

[9]G.W.R. Act, 1835.

failed their contract. This was then tendered out to Mr. Brewer of Rudloe, who worked in strict conjunction with Burge himself, whilst the ill-fated Mr. Lewis undertook some of the work from the Box end of the tunnel. Work began in earnest again in July 1838 with a three-year completion date imposed on the contractors, but increased steam power was agreed upon to augment the manual labour and so facilitate the deadline. Intense effort was then applied to the tunnel. Three hundred horses were used to drag up the earth and lime from the tunnel, some 40 boys to drive the horses and, as Thomas Gale again mentions 'as many as 1,100 or 1,200 men continually working, day and night'. There were 26 Inspectors on the site; some of these were despatched to keep the peace in the nearby villages on Sundays, there being no County police force at the time. In the last six months of work, no less than 4,000 men were feverishly engaged in finishing the job. Box and Corsham were transformed into temporary dormitory villages for the shift-workers, whilst local labour from Bath and North Wiltshire was recruited on even greater proportions.

The visit of James Tunstall, M.D. to the tunnel works in 1839 gives some impression of the Herculean activity:

We descended in the workmen's 'skid', covered with mud; immense blocks of stone lay in confused heaps; water dropped around; swarthy men were employed, some in laying the masonry, others in hewing the rocks; trucks lay in confused heaps, picturesquely lit by, here and there, a candle; whilst immense discharges, as of artillery, reverberated around.[10]

Accidents were luckily infrequent after the 1837 flood. There was another inflow of water in November 1838, but this was successfully cleared within ten days. *The Wiltshire Independent*, however, recorded a near-tragedy with more human consequences.

A few weeks ago, a man was about to 'fire a shot', that is, to blow up a piece of rock: he had prepared the hole for the charge, and was in the act of pouring gunpowder into it from an iron canister, containing about 20 pounds, which he held under his arm, when a drop of water having fallen from the roof upon the wick of his candle—most imprudently placed close by the hole—a spark flew from it into the powder, causing a most terrific explosion. The canister was burst to atoms, but not one piece entered the un-

[10] J. Tunstall: *Rambles about Bath and its Neighbourhood*, p. 274.

fortunate man who held it; he was dreadfully scorched, his clothes were torn off, his hair and eyebrows completely destroyed and his skin burned off all round his body; but... his eyesight was uninjured, and, although from the action of the flames he was miserably wounded and disfigured, he is now in a fair way of recovery.

The moment of highest tension arrived in July 1839. *The Wiltshire Independent* of 11th July 1839:

But, on breaking through the last intervening portion of rock, the accuracy of the headings was proved, and to the joy of the workmen, who took a lively interest in the result and to the triumph of Messrs. Lewis and Brewer's scientific working, it was found that the junction was perfect to A HAIR AS TO THE LEVEL, the entire roof forming an unvarying line; while laterally, the utmost deviation from a straight line was only ONE INCH AND A QUARTER!

The accuracy was indeed astonishing—it was so straight that on two days in the year, the sun could be seen shining through the tunnel. And so a project of immense enterprise was completed. Brunel is given the credit in the history books—a certain amount is his due. But the contractors must not be overlooked—it was their perseverance, coupled with the tremendous physical sacrifices of the ordinary workmen which enabled Brunel's planning to come to fruition. One mile, 1,452 yards in length, the tunnel was formed by clearing 247,000 cubic yards of material through 11 shafts, the deepest of which was some 293 feet below the level of the hill. One ton of candles had been burned each week and one ton of gunpowder and 20 million bricks required between 1838 and 1841.

The ultimate construction of Box Tunnel completed the line between Bath and Chippenham. But, in the previous year, on 31st August, 1840, came the first eventful day for Bath—the grand opening of the 12-mile section of line to Bristol, with a service of 10 trains each way on weekdays and four on Sundays. (For this journey the fare (single) was 2s. 6d. first-class and 1s. 6d. second.) The ceremonies were attended by huge crowds—bells were rung and guns fired. Twenty trips were run each way on that day alone by the four available engines to cater for those who wanted to sample the first delights of rail travel.

People's early fears of railways had been somewhat waived by their enthusiastic zeal for novelty—a natural human reaction. But the opening of the whole line on 31st July, 1841 (see Appendix), accompanied by equal pomp and ceremony, was more than a turning-point in Bath's history. No bands would play for the Turnpike Trust or the Canal Company—unless the tune was the Funeral March. Their receipts were irreprievably scythed. Not even the Canal Company's economy drive of 1842 or the Trust's decision to collect their tolls themselves could bring about a reversal of fortunes.

Bath had been swept into a new age, but the current was perhaps a little too fierce for some, who preferred to sample the beauty of England in more 'conventional' modes of transport:

However convenient the railway may be for travelling, it certainly has done away with much of its poetry. What can be more delightful than a drive on the now almost-forgotten stage, behind four high-bred horses, through the village scenery of England? But the train will not wait, so we must defer our romance until we have a hole drilled in our return-ticket.[11]

[11] J. Tunstall: Rambles about Bath and its Neighbourhood.

Sources

The Bath Turnpike Trust Acts, 1707–8, 1720–21, 1756–59 (Bath Reference Library).

The Act to complete, alter and enlarge the Kennet and Avon Canal, 1805 (Bath Reference Library).

The Great Western Railway Act, 1835 (Bath Reference Library).

A. Robertson: *A Topographical Survey of the Great Road from London to Bath and Bristol* (1792).

J. Tunstall: *Rambles about Bath and its Neighbourhood* (1847).

The Minute Book of the Bath Turnpike Trust, 1830–39 (Taunton County Records Office).

Two Scrapbooks of Newscuttings, Broadsheets and Small Posters relating to Bath Affairs (Bath Reference Library).

T. Gale: *A Brief Account of the Making and Working of the Great Box Tunnel* (1884).

C. G. Harper: *The Bath Road* (1889).

R. N. Worth: *A Tourist's Guide to Somersetshire* (1888).

M. Searle: *Turnpikes and Toll-Bars*.

K. R. Clew: *The Kennet and Avon Canal* (1968).

R. Athill: *Old Mendip* (1964).

Bath Chronicle.

The Bath Journal.

The Wiltshire Independent.

CHAPTER SEVEN

Bath and its New Local Government

DAVID DETHRIDGE

THOUGH from the earliest times Bath had claimed the status of a Corporation by prescriptive right, Elizabeth I granted a charter formally incorporating the City on 4th September, 1590, which in spite of an intermission in the 1680's, formed the basis of the constitution of Bath in the period up to 1835. The charter provided for a mayor elected annually by the Council, while the aldermen (numbering not less than four nor more than ten) and the twenty councillors were to hold office for life (unless removed), with vacancies to be filled by nomination from the Council.

The Corporation was empowered to make bye-laws and fix penalties (fines or imprisonment) for their contravention, and was given the duty to appoint a suitably qualified Recorder and a Common Clerk and Prothonotary. There were also to be two Bailiffs elected annually as well as a Chamberlain and two Sergeants-at-Mace. New boundaries for the city were fixed. Provision was made for a Court of Record, a prison, powers of arrest, assizes of bread, wine and beer, a view of frankpledge, and for the mayor to act as Coroner. Two of the aldermen were to be Justices. The Corporation was charged with the execution of particular statutes.

On 12th February, 1794, George III, in accord with the practice of granting modifications to charters following requests by Corporations, permitted the Mayor and the Recorder to appoint a deputy in the event of their illness or absence—a Deputy Mayor was to be chosen from the aldermen or justices. There were to be from four to nine additional justices, and provision was made for the protection of the hot springs and baths.

Who under this system composed the Corporation? The Royal

79

Commission on Municipal Corporations studied the appointment of councillors, concluding:

There is no principle of selection but that which arises from interest and connexion with the aldermen.

It was found to be the custom for newly appointed councillors to pay a fee of seven guineas to the Corporation. The number of aldermen was maintained at the maximum and any vacancies were automatically filled by the senior councilmen—a practice which prevails in many Borough and County authorities today. The Commissioners found that in all but two cases the mayor was chosen from the aldermen and that a principle of rotation had almost always been adhered to.

A bye-law was made on 15th March, 1808 requiring members to reside within a five-mile radius of the Guildhall, with removal from office the penalty for non-compliance. Though said to have been adopted owing to the absence of members, it was not invoked on any occasion.

The Corporations would naturally be expected to uphold the existing constitutional order: indeed Boroughs were the basis of the old Parliamentary system, their disfranchisement in 1832 being shortly followed by such reforming measures as the 1835 Act. The position of the Church of England, an integral part of the structure of government before Reform, was therefore the object of support by members of Bath's Corporation. A resolution 'in defence of the established Church' was passed in April 1807, petitions were sent to both Houses of Parliament 'against the claims of the Roman Catholics' in 1813, while in March 1821 a further petition was addressed to the legislature 'expressing their disappointment at the additional concessions being made to Roman Catholics'.

Nevertheless, the members of the Corporation realised that the constitution had become inadequate: when at the end of April in 1831 the Aldermen and Councillors re-elected Bath's two Members, Lord John Thynne and Major General Charles Palmer, unopposed, Mr. Norman in proposing the latter, 'a known advocate of reform' suggested that:

. . . If he had not supported that measure neither myself nor any of my colleagues would have desired to propose a man who had fled from his former profession of principle. I ask you not to keep the question of Reform out of view . . . vote for him because

80

he supported by his vote the grand measure of Reform [Cheers] which I firmly believe will be productive of the greatest good to the country. It cannot be argued with any degree of propriety, that however respectable the thirty members of this Corporation may be—however eligible be the persons they return to parliament —and however honest the motives for so returning them—it cannot be argued, I repeat that under any circumstances it is just that thirty men should have to act for the whole of this populous and important city. [Tremendous cheering]—and I verily believe it will be the means of repairing the pillars of the Constitution, which have been subject to the injuries of the devasting hand of time [Cheers]. I believe that the projected reformed representation will enable this country to maintain her high position among the nations of the earth, and save the Crown from the inroads of anarchy and confusion . . .

That those who benefited from the old system were prepared to reform it when it became necessary suggests that the Corporations before reform were not as far removed from public opinion as its detractors might claim.

REFORM

The Reform Commissioners prefaced their report on the 'corporation system' with the following passage:

We therefore feel it to be our duty to represent to Your Majesty, that the existing Municipal Corporations of England and Wales neither possess nor deserve the confidence or respect of your subjects; and that a thorough reform must be effected before they can become what we humbly submit to Your Majesty they ought to be, useful and efficient units of local government . . .

It was complained by the *Bath Chronicle* of 6th August, 1835 that the Commissioners were biased. The *Chronicle* adopted the view of the House of Lords, that while acknowledging the necessity of Reform 'they object to the wholesale and headlong manner in which the Government are dealing with this measure'.

Following their report, the Municipal Corporations Act was passed. As far as the composition of borough corporations was concerned, the authority was to consist mainly of popularly elected councillors, who would serve for three years and one third of their number would be elected each year. However, as a compromise with

81

the House of Lords, aldermen numbering one-third of the councillors were co-opted for six years, one half retiring every third year. This was intended to preserve to some extent the feature of continuity of the old system. In the case of the first aldermen and councillors, in order to bring the rotation of members into operation, only a part served the full term. The mayor was elected annually by the corporation.

The old Bath Council discussed the scheme on 29th July, 1835, having received a suggestion from the Committee of Municipal Corporations that the Council should petition against the Bill. A request for funds was included. In reply to this the following resolution was passed unanimously by the Corporation:

> ... that this Corporation do Petition the House of Lords accordingly and that such Petition do embrace the following points, viz. the appointment by charter of the Petitioners for Life— the attempt to displace them without any specific charge against them and without an opportunity of defending themselves—their desire to concur in and to propose any Equitable Scheme for Municipal Reform—the inexpediency of placing the Corporate Estates under the Control of persons without the proper Qualification, and giving such persons the power of levying Rates on the Inhabitants—The Inconvenience attending the frequency of the Election of Town Councillors—the Protection of the rights and Interests of the Freemen of the City—the propriety of continuing the power of licensing Public Houses in the Justices, and the protection of the Lessees for Lives of Corporate Property in the tenure of the same, and the right of renewing their Leases.

The petition was duly drawn up and approved and it was given to the Recorder, Marquess Camden, for presentation to the House of Lords. The Corporation decided not to contribute to the Committee's funds 'as they do not oppose the principle, but some of the details of the Measure'. Thus the Corporation's attitude to the Reform was quite moderate and reasoned. It may be added that the Maud Report on local government reorganisation considers that the existing system of annual partial elections should be replaced by triennial general elections, thus upholding the opinion expressed by Bath in 1835.

A meeting of the inhabitants of Bath, in which about one thousand people took part, favoured the Reform, although the *Bath Chronicle* noted the lack of 'substantial inhabitants and respectable trades-men', who, thought the paper, would have been present had the Bill received as much support as its proponents claimed.

The first elections under the new system provided an opportunity for members of the old corporation to submit themselves—and in a sense the old system—to the judgment of the electors. Of the forty-two new councillors, chosen from eighty-six candidates, six were retiring members: Councillors Lye, Savage and Tugwell had been common council men and Kitson, Phillott (an Elizabethan Justice) and Norman had been aldermen—the last mentioned being the retiring mayor and the presiding members at the first meeting of the reformed council.

Great care was taken, as the vote of thanks to those who took the 'conciliating measures' shows, to secure an agreed selection of the first aldermen. The seven to hold office for six years were chosen from the councillors, and of these two were former aldermen—Messrs. Norman and Phillott. The other five were new councillors. None of the remaining seven either were or had been councillors; nor did any of them have the same surname as any of the present or retiring councillors.

FREEMEN

Though the term originally meant, according to the Reform Commissioners, all those who were not vassals, the Charter of Elizabeth conferred upon the corporation the exclusive right to create freemen. The Commissioners gave their account of how this power was exercised:

> They afterwards, for their own emolument, sold the city freedom and divided the money, keeping the number as few as possible that the purchase money might be increased.

The only ways in which freedom could be obtained were by servitude and purchase. Servitude required, amongst other things, an apprenticeship to a freeman who either lived or worked within the old limits of the city. The total fees paid on admission to freedom by servitude were £2 7s. 0d. The council was empowered— or acted as though it were—to fix the amount required for purchase of freedom. This increased from ten guineas in 1733 to £75 in 1801, to £100 in 1802 and to 100 guineas in 1803. In 1805 a figure of 120 guineas was laid down, which became 250 guineas in 1810. In

addition a fee of £5 was payable. The Commissioners remarked that:
The Charter says not a word about selling freedoms. This is an
abuse to put money in the pocket of the Corporation. No usage
can sanctify such a mode of filling up the Corporation Offices and
pockets at the same time.

It was usual for the councillors to be chosen from those who had
obtained their freedom by purchase; many of the purchases took
place on the eve of the election. Of the thirty members of the
corporation in 1834, twenty-five had purchased their freedom and
of the remainder, four had been apprenticed to medical practitioners
and the fifth to a baker. On this the report says: 'Of the five members
mentioned as having obtained their freedom by servitude, four were
apprenticed to their own fathers, who were Aldermen—that is
Tudor, Spry, Kitson and Phillott. The Baker apprenticeship excited
some risibility in the Court both from the Commissioners and
audience.'

There was an estate in whose profits the resident freemen—who in
1831 numbered 104—shared. A bye-law of 1646 restricted the right
to open shops to freemen, on pain of a fine of five shillings for each
week. In the report it was said not to have been enforced within
living memory. However, the appendix to the report added that
'This usurpation was not abandoned till its successful opposition, in
a Court of Justice, by a person named Glazeby, a tailor, in the year
1765, who shivered to atoms the monopoly of these pseudo and
fraudulent guilds'. It was said that there had in the previous century
been companies of traders, but the Commissioners found no trace of
them.

One of the most notable opponents of the differentials of citizens
was Thomas Paine. In the *Rights of Man* he declares:
The country is cut up into monopolies. Every chartered town
is an aristocratical monopoly in itself . . . Within these monopolies
there are other monopolies. In a city, such for instance as Bath,
which contains between twenty and thirty thousand inhabitants,
the right of electing representatives to Parliament is monopolised
into about 31 persons.

But though the new system was based upon the conception of the
'undifferentiated citizen', a meeting in June 1835 at the Greyhound
Inn of the freemen of Bath, excluding members of the Corporation,
unanimously supported the Municipal Reform Bill.

OFFICERS OF THE CORPORATION

After the composition of the Corporation, its officers and servants, its charitable work and other services should be dealt with. The Reform Commissioners referred to 'Nominal offices, obtained by intrigue, meanness and too often by the vilest practices'.

There was a Recorder who held office during good behaviour. There was no residence qualification. The holder of the office at the time of the report was Marquess Camden, whose father had been the previous holder. The report observed that Elizabeth's charter required the Recorder to be 'learned in law', but when the Corporation wanted to appoint a tory noble, they consulted a lawyer who informed them that since the House of Lords constituted a court, peers were in fact 'learned in law'. Since the Corporation were unable to find a Deputy Recorder—the power of appointing a deputy was never exercised—people had to travel 50 miles in search of justice.

From the Chamberlain's and Treasurer's Accounts it is possible to compare salaries and wages before and after the reform. The figures used here are those for 1832 to 1833 and 1841 to 1842. The Mayor's old salary of £1,000 had become £200. The Town Clerk received £400 rather than £500. The Hallkeeper (who became Hallkeeper and Crier) was paid £80 instead of £60. The Chamberlain was paid £400, but the Treasurer, who replaced him, was only paid £300, although his salary reached £400 by 1846. The salary of a Sergeant-at-Mace dropped from £200 to £130. The Mayor's Officers received a total of £109 4s. 0d. in 1842 as opposed to £273 in 1833.

SERVICES

The amount spent on the various services in the 1833 and 1842 accounts do not indicate much significant change in continued services. For example, in 1832 to 1833 £96 9s. 3d. was spent in the Baths and Pump Room. The figure for 1841 to 1842 was £70 12s. 10d., but between then and 1847 the expenditure varied from £19 7s. 9d. in 1844 to 1845, to £128 4s. 4d. the following year. In general, variations in expenditure do not appear to be connected with the Reform.

However, new services were provided. The corporation discussed the deficiency of water on 8th January, 1836—its third meeting. Waterworks, as well as road improvements appear in the accounts for 1842.

The most notable new item is expenditure on the police, amounting to over five thousand pounds, although among the recipients of the 'subscriptions and donations' referred to below are organisations which performed what would be regarded as police functions. Part of the business of the third meeting was the appointment of a watch committee. (See Chapter Eight.)

The cost of the municipal elections which the reform introduced was £157 2s. 6d. between 1841 and 1842.

In 1833, £453 10s. 0d. was the total recorded for 'subscriptions and donations'. In addition £66 2s. 9d. was given to Bellott's Hospital, £250 12s. 6d. to the Grammar School and £9 3s. 8d. for bread for the Poor. The only comparable item in 1842 was 'Charities £8 15s. 0d.'. The same figure appeared in 1847. From this, it seems that the Commissioners' allegations of plunder were not a justifiable criticism of the old system.

The general financial position did not alter greatly. The allocation to annuities increased from £392 17s. 0d. to £745 2s. 0d. Entertainments, on which £86 15s. 0d. was spent between 1832 and 1833, disappeared.

CONCLUSIONS

The extreme statements of the Commissioners and their forceful language do not seem to be justified. To them the 'Corporation system' was discredited. In contrast, the Public Committee of Manchester Citizens, which led the reform movement in that city, desired the incorporation of Manchester under a close body:

> We conceive that a permanent body of guardians of the peace, clothed with the authority of the magistracy, would here, as in other places, be the natural guardian of all interior public interests, able to conduct them with uniformity and consistency, and ready at all times for the immediate prevention or correction of abuses, and might represent the Inhabitants in all their external relations with a character and dignity becoming the largest provincial community in the United Kingdom.

Certainly it was not difficult to find fault with the old system. Bath Corporation accepted that some reform was necessary. What is significant about the Manchester report is that it wished to 'obtain reforms' and considered that a permanent body was the best means of 'correcting abuses'.

The transition was accomplished without upheaval. The fears expressed by the Corporation concerning the placing of corporate property in new hands proved to be groundless. The establishment of an elective Corporation was the logical extension of the Parliamentary reform.

Sources

Sources: (all primary sources in Bath City Record Office).
Charters of the City of Bath from 1189.
Council Minutes from 1631.
Chamberlain's Accounts, 1832–35.
Treasurer's Accounts, 1842–47.
Answers on the Corporation Bill to both Houses (1789).
S. and B. Webb: *The Development of English Local Government, 1689–1835.*
J. H. Warren: *The English Local Government System.*

CHAPTER EIGHT

Law and Order in Bath

MARK ROBERTS and JOHN WROUGHTON

ONE of the aspects of local government investigated by the Commissioners on Municipal Corporations when they visited Bath, was the policing and watching of the city. By the end of 1835, Bath had a system which was partly enlightened, but largely disorganised. The city, in fact, was patrolled not by one police force, but by three! Each force had different powers; each was independent of the other two. The whole borough was therefore protected with the exception, as we shall see, of Lyncombe and Widcombe—two of the most needy areas.

The central part of Bath (i.e. the old city parishes of St. Peter and St. Paul, St. Michael and St. James) was regulated by a Police Act of 1814, which replaced an earlier Act of 1766. Under its terms, a body of twenty-three commissioners, elected by the Corporation and parish vestries, was made responsible for 'paving, cleansing, lighting, watching, regulating and improving the city of Bath'.

By 1835 the effect of this Improvement Commission on the policing of the old city area was clearly evident. A large and fairly effective force of two inspectors, six night constables and seventy-two watchmen had been recruited to patrol the streets *at night*.[1] Divided into three companies, they received instructions to 'prevent fires, murders, burglaries, robberies and other outrages and disorders' and powers to 'apprehend all night walkers, malefactors and suspected persons, who shall be found wandering or misbehaving themselves'. Each night constable was responsible for his own team of watchmen and was required to tour round the streets at intervals to check on their presence. He was also obliged to record any

[1] *Report of Commissioners on Municipal Corporations, 1835.*

incidents in a book, which was to be taken to the Mayor's office for inspection by eleven o'clock each morning. Failure to comply with these instructions could result in a fine of twenty shillings. Fully aware of the weakness of human nature, the Act also threatened a fine of five pounds on any publican who entertained watchmen or constables during their hours of duty.[2]

The duties of this force, however, were purely confined to the 'nightly watch'; they had no powers to act as a 'day police'. In this old area of the city, day-time enforcement of law and order was traditionally the responsibility of the five Mayor's officers, under the nominal control of the two Chief Constables (who were members of the Common Council). Appointed personally by the Mayor, the officers were required to attend the local courts, to execute warrants and to preserve the peace of the city. The Head Officer was paid twenty-five shillings a week, whilst his deputies each received a guinea.

During times of emergency they could call on additional officers known as Tithingmen, who were only paid when actually on duty. By 1835 there were a hundred and thirty of these Tithingmen, although the office was fast becoming obsolete with the arrival of a new type of 'crisis' police. The Special Constables Act of 1831, introduced at the time of the Reform Bill riots, gave to local justices the power to conscript men as special constables in cases of civil upheaval. Bath speedily took advantage of these extra powers when, on Sunday, 30th October, 'groups of the lowest rabble collected at the White Hart' to demonstrate in favour of reform. (See Chapter Two.) Three hundred special constables were called in to disperse the mob. On 4th November the Mayor, for fear of any further disturbance, issued notices inviting citizens to enrol as special constables. The city was divided into four 'grand divisions', which were further split into twenty-one 'districts'. Each district, under a superintendent, had its own little force of special constables. Patrols operated in the streets from 6 p.m. each evening and were relieved every four hours. Bath survived the crisis. The authorities, clearly delighted at the response to their appeal for recruits, issued the following statement:

> The magistrates are highly gratified by the zeal and energy evinced by all classes of the inhabitants in aid of the Civil Power, in the protection of property and preservation of the peace.

[2]City Police Act, 54 Geo. III (1814).

But the special constable was only a temporary expedient in times of crisis. By 1835 the old part of the city still lacked an efficient and permanent day-time police force. The Parliamentary Commissioners, who reported on Bath in that year, noted that 'the chairmen are sometimes sworn in as special constables, but are not found very effective'.

In the meantime, the parish of Walcot had established its own police force, which was remarkably efficient and progressive. The Walcot Police Act of 1793 had set up a force of night watchmen who, by a further Act of 1825, could also be sworn in as regular day-time constables. Mainwaring commented on the effectiveness of this system. Whereas in 1792 Walcot was 'incommodious and unsafe for passengers, being very ill-paved and not sufficiently cleansed, lighted and watched', in 1825 'an effective police was established and the hordes of beggars which daily infested the streets speedily removed'.[3] A further step forward was taken in 1830 when the whole force was re-modelled on the pattern of Peel's newly created Metropolitan Police. Its organisation, methods and uniform were made almost identical to those of the London Force. The top hat, blue frock coat with brass buttons, blue trousers and cape soon became familiar to the people of Walcot. It had the distinction of being one of the first places in the country outside the capital to have a properly organised police system. It was placed under the control of twenty-two commissioners, all wealthy property owners, who were elected at the parish vestry every four years.

The Walcot day-time force was made up of four divisions, each containing from between nine and fifteen constables who were responsible to an inspector of police. Each constable was allocated two beats out of the nine in each division and was on duty for periods of between four and eight hours. The day patrols began at 8 a.m., finishing at midnight. The night force then took over with three companies of night watchmen and night constables, each under the control of an inspector. For a night's work, a constable received three shillings and a watchman one shilling and fourpence. The duty inspectors of both forces recorded their experiences in a remarkably illiterate and perfunctory way, but their report books provide a valuable insight into the tenor of disorder in Bath at this time.

The amount of crime reported by Inspector John Withers of 'D' division between 12th May, 1835 and 19th November, 1835 was

[3]R. Mainwaring: *Annals of Bath*, pp. 334–35.

quite small in scale, but frequent in nature.[4] Early in May the attempt of thieves to break into No. 7 Lower East Hay dwelling house was frustrated by a secure lock, while in June the police disturbed some robbers at Claremont Place who only managed to steal a pair of stockings and a pair of stays left in the garden to dry. Later in June, 'some person did contrive to take a portable desk and between sixty and seventy pounds in sovereigns' from Mr. Wieldbroun of 21 Park Street. Again the culprits would appear to be raw amateurs. Very little crime was of an organised nature, but committed rather in the desperation of the moment.

On August 31st 1835 at half-past-six in the evening Mr. Jeff's servant at number six St. James's Square, let in a young man of very bad character to give him something to eat and drink. The consequence was that he contrived to steal the servant's silver watch, gold seal and two keys attached, four silver forks, two salt spoons and one teaspoon, the property of Mr. Jeffs.

The only other successful theft of real note took place between six and eight o'clock on the evening of 15th November, 1835 when Mr. Butcher of Nelson Place had his home broken into and a pocket book, some sovereigns and two silver salt spoons stolen. A degree of expertise and cunning was shown by the thieves, who entered the front door by means of a false key while the family was at church.

The keynote in 1835 seems to have been the undramatic nature of most of the crime. The Inspectors similarly find little to complain of in the conduct of the police constables. Their record was blotted, however, by the common misdemeanour of over-drinking. On 16th June, 1835 Inspector Withers reported Jos England for returning to his office at twelve o'clock at night drunk. Nevertheless, the police received considerable respect from the public and seldom met interference in their duty. The only such incident occurred on 3rd August, 1835 when Job Lucas was summoned by Inspector Withers for attempting to rescue a prisoner from him. Lucas appeared to the summons and was fined forty shillings to cover costs. In general the constable's main efforts were directed towards ensuring that all area gates were firmly closed at night.

Earlier, in the years 1832–33, life does not seem to have been quite so passive for the police force, and greater initiative was required to

[4]*Walcot Police Duty Inspector's Report Book, No.*[1] —'*D*' *Division.*

apprehend the criminals and detect the crimes.[5] In 1832 there were three outstanding cases of robbery. On 31st January the home of Mr. Little, a draper and tailor at Cleveland Place, was entered by the workshop window. Mr. Little awoke and alarmed the thieves who made off leaving behind seventeen keys and a crow bar. Inspector Hillman and Constable Wright received fulsome praise for their conduct from Mr. Little who discovered that nothing was missing except for three silver table spoons and a few teaspoons. A familiar petty theft interested the police on 14th June when the Brittania public house was entered and thirty shillings in copper and four silver spoons stolen. The most serious theft of the year, however, struck the home of Mr. Hobbes at 10 Park Street, when forty sovereigns and one ten pound note together with a quantity of plate and jewelry to the value of one hundred and fifty pounds were stolen from a Madame Latrouche who was there in lodging.

Most clearly the years following the close of the Napoleonic wars were times of distress and hunger. Many petty thefts were certainly motivated by the need to feed and clothe a wife and family. On 10th February, 1833 a shop in Northampton Buildings was the scene for such a crime. A scavenger stole a four pound piece of beef from the shop, and was subsequently apprehended. The case was clear against him since the daughter of the proprietor, Mrs. Bence, saw him take it from the shelf, but from human sympathy, and the beef being found, she would not appear against him. On 23rd December, 1832, the inspector of 'C' division was proceeding on his rounds where he saw Little 'regularly going over his beat'. Suddenly there was a great noise as a soldier ran away with a pair of ducks from the Brittania public house. He was seized by the inspector and Constable Little but was saved by the interference of his father and several others.

On balance, therefore, Walcot was extremely fortunate in the state of its police force. From 1801 the parish of Bathwick, too, had had its own force of night watchman (much on the lines of the city force), but with no day-time patrols. The Commissioners of the three areas mentioned—the city, Walcot and Bathwick—were also responsible for the paving and lighting of the streets (which clearly assisted the work of the police). In 1818 they obtained an Act to establish the Bath Gas Light and Coke Company, with a contract to supply their parishes with street lamps. These were in operation by

[5] *Walcot Police Duty Inspector's Report Book, 1832–33—'C' Division.*

1819. Those parts of Walcot not included in the original Act, were lit by the Walcot Police Act of 1825. For these services of paving, lighting and watching the ratepayers of the city parishes paid 8d. in the pound, those of Walcot 10d., and those of Bathwick one shilling.

On the surface, at least, Bath seemed to be well in advance of most cities in providing those conditions necessary for the maintenance of law and order. But one serious gap remained. The parish of Lyncombe and Widcombe, just on the other side of the river, had no police force at all. The Parliamentary Commissioners who visited the city in 1835 underlined the stupidity of this situation:

> The parts of Lyncombe and Widcombe which are near the bridge are very densely inhabited, and a great number of small houses have been built there within a few years. Great inconvenience is stated to arise from the Bath police having no power to go beyond the bridge, and disturbances are said to arise on that side of the bridge in consequence of there being no regulation for lighting it.

They went on to recommend strongly that the three police forces should be amalgamated with their powers extended to include Lyncombe and Widcombe. The area involved, they argued, would by no means be too extensive for one board of commissioners to control. At the moment the three forces were treading too frequently on each other's toes for full efficiency to be maintained. The report significantly hinted its approval of the Walcot system. 'It is found to be very effective.' This, they clearly felt, was the model for the future.

Bath did not have to wait long for a chance to put these recommendations into practice. The Municipal Corporations Act of 1835, taking full heed of the reports of the Parliamentary Commissioners, directed that each borough should elect a Watch Committee to establish and administer a permanent police force, the cost of which was to be met out of the local rates. Although the Watch Committee would have the power to appoint, suspend and dismiss constables, it would remain under the authority of the Home Secretary to whom it was obliged to send quarterly reports.

Bath again demonstrated its progressive outlook by responding both quickly and enthusiastically to these proposals. By 1836 the city had set up an amalgamated force to cover all areas (including Lyncombe and Widcombe) by day and by night. This was certainly not the case on the national level. By 1838 only half the boroughs had established police forces and even by 1845 thirty boroughs had failed to comply. Bath, of course, already had a firm foundation in the old Walcot Police—and it was on this that the new system was built.

The Bath Watch Committee was appointed on 8th January, 1836. It wasted no time in setting about its tasks.[6] A letter was written almost immediately to Colonel Rowan, the Chief Commissioner of the London Police, to ask for a copy of their regulations and for any advice he could give on setting up the new Bath Force. Two sub-committees were formed—one to investigate the problem of Lyncombe and Widcombe; the other to work out the 'take-over' of the old forces. On 11th January, Captain William Carroll, R.N., was appointed Chief Constable at a salary of 'not less than £200'. A notice was placed outside the Guildhall inviting applicants 'not exceeding forty years of age' to join the new force. The sub-committee reported back, having toured the old police areas, and recommended the following number of beats for the amalgamated force:

	Beats	Constables for day	Constables for night	Total Men
Bath	26	10	52	62
Walcot ..	12	6	22	28
Bathwick ..	6	3	15	18
TOTAL	44	19	89	108

The full Committee met on 19th January and submitted to the City Council their final scheme for the size and cost of the force. They hastened to reassure the Council that the scale of wages was 'the lowest for which an efficient constabulary force can be formed'. They warned them, however, that the figures given below did not include the cost of uniforms, providing the Chief Constable with an office or extending the system to Lyncombe and Widcombe:

[6]Material for the following paragraphs is taken from the *Bath Watch Committee Minute Book, 1836–43.*

	£	s.	d.
1 Chief Constable—not less than	200	0	0
2 Superintendents at 31s. 6d. per week ..	163	16	0
10 Inspectors at £1 1s. 0d. per week	546	0	0
100 Constables at 15s. per week	3900	0	0
Total:	4809	16	0

Meeting now almost daily, the Watch Committee proceeded with its work at a breathtaking pace. A house at 10 Kingston Buildings was taken for the Chief Constable's office at a rent of £24 per annum. The Lyncombe and Widcombe sub-committee produced an estimate of £600 per annum as the cost of providing police and street lighting for that area. (Constables would be provided, in the meantime, with lamps until the street lighting was ready.) Captain Carroll busied himself by drawing up proposed rules and regulations for the new force. In general status and appearance it was to differ very little from the pattern of the old Walcot police. On 29th January, for instance, the Committee ordered that an advertisement be placed in the Bath papers for tenders for great coats, blue close coats, blue trousers, capes, hats and scarves *similar to those in use in the outpart of Walcot*. The first batch of constables was appointed on 29th January, measured for their uniforms on 8th February and commenced duty a week later.

Meanwhile, the Committee had accepted tenders for the new uniforms. William Hanham agreed to make the constable's great coat, close coat and trousers for £3 2s. 3d. a suit. (A hundred and thirty-two of these were ordered, presumably taking account of the additional constables needed for Lyncombe and Widcombe.) The Inspector's uniform was to cost £4 6s. 6d. In each case, the suits were 'to be made of cloth not inferior to the sample now produced, and such suits to include a plated button having on it the Bath arms of the Police Force'. Hanham was also to provide one hundred and forty-six capes at 8s. 6d. each with 'a strap and button at the neck, and a button to secure the cape in front'. Top hats were to be supplied by George Cox at a cost of 14s. each. Later, the Chief Constable was allowed £12 16s. 2d. to purchase 'a hundred staves for the constables with swivels at the end for the ties'. In March it was agreed, at Captain Carroll's suggestion, that the uniform should be modified for the summer months. Each constable was to be provided with a pair of duck trousers at a cost not exceeding five shillings, but the constable himself was to provide another pair. A year later (3rd July, 1837) the cost of police uniforms had gone up considerably, judging by this estimate from a Mr. Hamper (which was accepted):

(*a*) *Police Officers:*

	£	s.	d.
Great coat complete	1	19	0
Close coat	1	11	0
Cotton embroidered		2	6
Trousers		17	6
Armlets			11
Total	£4	10	11

(*b*) *Police Inspectors:*

	£	s.	d.
Inspector's close coat and trousers	2	18	0
Great coat	2	14	0
Cotton close coat		2	6
Total	£5	14	6

An eternal problem for the committee seems to have been the difficulty in finding suitable human material for the force. All too often Watch Committees were forced, or found it an easy way out, to recruit inferior men from existing night watchmen. The number of dismissals for bad conduct in the early stages testifies to this problem. In the year 1837 there were no less than twenty-four dismissals, but in 1841 there were only three. A rigid code of personal behaviour was inflicted upon the police constables. Not only were no associations, societies, or combinations to be formed by the police force without the express sanction of the Watch Committee, but in August 1837 the Committee supported Captain Carroll in preventing police officers from partaking of any entertainment. This, they hoped, would 'ensure the independence and impartiality of the police'. Above all, constables were not to fraternise with the public. The Committee were prompted on the 3rd November, 1837 to declare that any policeman found neglecting his duty by gossiping was liable to forefeit a sum not exceeding one day's pay. By 8th May, 1840, constables were to submit to the payment of a fine not exceeding ten shillings for improper conduct or neglect of duty. These were no idle threats. On 31st July, 1840, George Noles, a police constable, was charged by Inspector Tanner with being for a considerable time in 'conversation with common prostitutes on his beat, near the Hop Pole between eight and nine o'clock . . . and with drinking at the Hop Pole when he ought to have been on duty'. George Noles was instantly discharged from service.

A continual preoccupation of the Watch Committee was finance, and any means of reducing the size of the force, and yet maintaining law and order. Somewhat reluctantly on 3rd November, 1837 the Committee decided that it would be inexpedient to diminish the size of the police, even though the inhabitants of Widcombe and Lyncombe had expressed their distaste for the overbearing numbers of police patrolling the area. Finally, after comparing the expenses of the Bath Police with those of Bristol, Exeter and Leeds, on 15th June, 1838 Captain Carroll, chairman of the sub-committee, authorised the dismissal of twelve constables. But no sooner had the fourth quarterly report been sent to the Home Office on 28th September commending the reduced force, than an addition of fifty men was made necessary on 10th May, 1839 by the exigencies of Chartist riots. Once again in 1840 Captain Carroll was authorised to reduce the force, but the Mayor attended a meeting on 18th June, 1841 and stated that the magistrates desired an increase of thirty men for the ensuing election.

If the Watch Committee reports were honestly drawn up, then the police appear to have been generally respected for their conduct. The nature of their job made it inevitable that many should be reprimanded for minor offences of drunkenness. Working long hours for a low pay, the police constables' status was lower than that of his present day counterpart. However, despite the indiscretions of individuals, in the second quarterly report of the Watch Committee in April 1837 a favourable opinion was expressed of the efficiency of the police force and of its continued exertions for the purposes of its establishment. In troublesome times such as at the Quarter Sessions 'the peace of the city was secured and every facility afforded to render approaches to the court acceptable to all'; but, as among all human beings, there were some incidents of sheer idiocy. On the 24th June, 1836 William Sartam was charged by the inspector for having lent his police coat to one Moody, a discharged constable, in a public house 'who made an improper use of it by assuming the authority of a constable'. He was further charged with drunkenness and discharged from the service. William Gover and William King were charged by Charles Bowker on 19th August, 1836 with not aiding him in quelling a disturbance on Snow Hill. More seriously, on 2nd September, 1836 Henry Chiswell was reported by Captain Carroll for 'ill-treating an old man in the Gravel Walk and for disrespectful conduct towards the magistrates'. He was first suspended for his conduct and then dismissed for not attending the meeting to answer the charge.

Police constables only very rarely seem to have been involved in fights with members of the public, but when they were injured they did receive some help from the Committee. On 15th July, 1836 Joseph Elliot, a constable, received severe injury to his hand in a fire at Prior Park. Being disabled from duty, he was ordered to receive the sum of four pounds as compensation. A serious outbreak of violence required quelling by Thomas Withers on 15th February, 1836. He suppressed a fierce disturbance at the Bell in Stall Street but received a severe blow on the back part of his head. 'Being disabled by such injury in working for maintenance of himself, wife and four children', the Committee decided he should be allowed the sum of ten shillings per week for one year, and his re-recruitment should be subject to reconsideration.

Even the inspectors were not immune from punishment for malpractice. Inspector Withers was charged by Captain Carroll on 10th July, 1837. Apparently, he had received from Jacob Pound, a senior police officer, a female on a charge of stealing five shillings and half-a-crown from a gentleman. Withers found the money on the girl and returned it to the gentleman without making any entry of the charge. He was thereupon ordered to be suspended for one month, his previous good conduct acting in mitigation of his punishment.

At Christmas time, the constables were especially prone to getting drunk and also breaking the rule imposed by the Committee prohibiting officers from receiving sums of money in the form of Christmas boxes. (The public were, however, invited to contribute 'at this season of the year to the police benefit fund'.) Similarly, drinking in public houses, as a protracted rest from the beat, was continually condemned as lowering the general character of the police in the eyes of the public. On 14th August, 1837 Captain Carroll stated in committee that Inspector Thomas had complained of several policemen eating and drinking at the Dolphin, Broad Street. It was immediately recorded as the opinion of the Committee that 'whether on or off duty, constables should not be seen in public houses particularly in their uniforms'.

Sometimes the inspectors themselves fell out. Such an amusing incident took place on 1st November, 1839.

Inspector Hyatt complained of Inspector Bowker having on Sunday night last used violent and threatening language towards him in Station House, and having taken off his coat and put himself into an attitude of fighting with him.

The Committee ordered that Inspector Bowker be discharged from the service, he not having denied the charge.

In spite of these dismissals for bad conduct, the opinion of people living at the time seems to suggest that the Bath Police Force was both effective and appreciated. A citizen of Bath, replying to questions put to him in 1836 by the Royal Commission on Constabularies, said this:

When I lived four miles from Bath my property was injured and stolen. My house was broken into and other times attacked by robbers ... My nights, instead of seasons of refreshing rest, were times of careful and painful watching to guard against the midnight robber.

I now live in the borough of Bath. A day and night police is continually passing around my home. I am not annoyed with insolent beggars. I sleep securely undisturbed by robbers. I have no dread of thieves and my property is secured from the spoiler and thief.

The contrast in the two residences I feel to be as if I were removed from the abodes of savage society to live among a highly civilised and intellectual people.

That the efforts of the police were appreciated, was shown also by a letter to the *Bath Chronicle* in January 1843 which criticised the attempts being made to reduce the size of the force. The writer hoped that his fellow citizens 'will themselves take some steps for the security of their property, which is at present in much jeopardy from the false economy and impotent measures of the Watch Committee'. From 10 p.m. to 6 a.m., he complained, the safety of the city district and parishes of Widcombe, Walcot and Bathwick was confided to only forty men. The constables, too, did not get a fair deal—their average daily duty was not less than nine hours with the addition of three nights out of five; they often spent fourteen hours out of twenty-four on duty; even their shortest beat was over one mile in length. Whilst this letter is clearly critical of the administration of the Watch Committee, at least it reflects a feeling that the Bath Police Force was both wanted and necessary. In this city of propertied wealth, the police were regarded as the friends, not the foes of the people. Certainly the anti-police demonstrations, which occurred elsewhere in the country, did not happen here. Their quiet efficiency bred respect. Even the night watchmen of the old forces were never quite the laughing stock they seem to have been in other cities.

There were, of course, some complaints against the police—a complaint by the proprietor of the Greyhound Inn in 1841 that his house had not been 'sufficiently protected by the police during the late elections'; a complaint in 1838 against police constables Gibbs and Wells 'having been present in Union Street last Tuesday week at 4 a.m. and not having interfered to prevent a dog fight which continued for twenty minutes, and which they ought to have suppressed immediately'; a complaint, also in 1838, of noises in Union Street 'at very unreasonable hours by men and women of the town, and of the inattention of the police constables on such occasions'; a complaint by Mr. Clementson against Constable Powell 'having with a cane struck his son while running through Bath Street'.

On the whole, however, public relations were good. Most people would have joined the Watch Committee in its thanks to Captain Carroll in June 1836, 'for his unwearied asiduity and constant attention to the duties of his office ... not only in preserving the peace by day and by night, but in being pre-eminently accessory to the extinguishing of six distinct and separate fires which have occurred'. Indeed, fire-fighting—which had traditionally been part of the policeman's duties—provided the force with an excellent opportunity to impress the public. It is true that the Fire Insurance

Offices had their own fire engines with men trained to assist their clients. It is true also that by 1845 the Corporation had built a fire main in the centre of the city, from which 'leathern hoses' attached to fire-cocks would provide a continuous stream of water, which could be thrown over high buildings. But, according to a report in 1845, small fires were 'generally put out by the police, who are furnished with leather buckets by several offices'.[7] The Bath Police turned out in full force at the great fire at Prior Park School in 1836. According to Bishop Barnes, 'their conduct was above all praise'. Ninety constables worked furiously under the direction of the Chief Constable 'and there was not one single instance of inebriety, disorder, inattention or insubordination'.

The Watch Committee's thanks to Captain Carroll paid this final tribute to his work during the first four months of the new Police Force: 'As a further evidence of their exertions in the protection of property they have within the period of their services taken 203 persons into custody'. What exactly happened to people taken into custody? According to the report of the Commissioners on Municipal Corporations in 1835, 'disorderly persons' were first locked in one of the three watchhouses (in Walcot, Bathwick and the Market-place) before being taken to the local magistrate. The magistrates had the power to punish all minor offences, including assaults. The Bath Court of Quarter Sessions did very little business at this time, because it was not allowed to try felonies. This was regarded as a great disadvantage:

> With a population exceeding 50,000 persons in the city and immediate neighbourhood, the most trifling cases of larceny must be sent to be tried at the County Quarter Sessions or Assizes, which are held at Wells, Bridgwater and Taunton, at the distance of 18, 39 and 50 miles from Bath.

All prisoners committed by the magistrates to hard labour were sent to the county house of correction at Shepton Mallet. It was estimated that about 200 prisoners were sent there each year, including vagrants.

Bath's other local court was the Court of Requests which met every Wednesday to hear cases of debt. With an average of eighty new cases a week, it was extremely busy. Between March 1833 and March 1835, 350 people were committed to Bath City Gaol for

[7] *Report of Commissioners into the State of Large Towns, 1845.*

101

debts ranging from 2s. 9½d. to £10. The standard periods of imprisonment were 20 days for debts under £1, 40 days under £2, 60 days under £3, 80 days under £4, 100 days under £5 and 200 days under £10. The City Gaol, situated in Bathwick,[8] was under the care of a gaoler (who received £120 per annum), a surgeon and a chaplain (who each received 50 guineas). Guard duty was performed by the police. The Gaol was normally used to house debtors and minor offenders, each of whom was allowed a diet of one and a half pounds of bread daily. For the years 1832–34 the minor offences carrying prison sentences included breach of the peace (62 cases), exposing fruit for sale on footways (63 cases), assault (8 cases), bastardy (3 cases), keeping a disorderly house (2 cases). 31 of these offenders were under 18 years of age, the youngest being 14 years. Sentences ranged from 7 to 40 days for exposing fruit for sale on the footways, with 184 days as the longest for a breach of the peace.[9]

Bath in the Age of Reform found itself well-prepared to deal with the threatened upheavals of a turbulent period. Although it can be argued that Bath, lacking large industrial populations, was not a natural breeding ground for crime, it was nevertheless a major centre of radical opinion. It is therefore, much to its credit that it passed through the crisis of Parliamentary Reform, the crisis of Chartism and the crisis of the Anti-Corn Law League unscathed by serious riots, unmarred by bloodshed. Backed by the enthusiasm of a propertied class (anxious no doubt, to protect its own interests), Bath in the provinces led the way in the search for law and order. As a city it was amongst the first to establish Improvement Commissions (1766), amongst the first to copy Peel's London 'Bobbies', (1830), and amongst the first to set up a full-time Police Force under the terms of the Municipal Corporations Act (1836).

The Bath Police Force, costing nearly £5,000 a year to run, was largely untrained. It was certainly over-worked. Judging from the number of dismissals, it probably attracted the wrong sort of men. But it was sufficiently well-disciplined, enthusiastic and efficient to meet with the approval of the citizens. Petty crime—caused largely by the grinding poverty of the poorer classes—abounded. Much of it doubtless went undetected. It is perhaps significant, however, that major crimes found little place in the report books either before 1836 or after. Bath, unlike some cities, was accustomed to having

[8]In Grove Street.
[9]*Report on the Condition of Bath Gaol, 1835.*

its police around, thanks to the foundations laid by the old Walcot, Bathwick and City Forces. (It is significant that the only murmurings against the new set-up came from Lyncombe and Widcombe—areas not used to the tread of the constable's boots!) For the most part, hardened criminals kept away or lurked in the shadows. The honest citizen paid his watch rate gratefully—and then saw to it that he got value for money!

Sources

Walcot Police Duty Inspector's Report Book, 1832–33 and 1835 (Bath City Record Office).

Bath Watch Committee Minute Book, 1836–43 (Bath City Record Office).

Report of Commissioners on Municipal Corporations, 1835 (British Museum, H.C. (1835) Vol. XXIV).

Report on the Condition of Bath Gaol, 1835 (British Museum H.C. (1835) Vol. XIV).

City Police Act, 54 Geo. III (British Museum, Local Acts (1814) c. cv).

Walcot Police Act, 6 Geo. IV (British Museum, Local Acts (1825) c. lxxiv).

Bathwick Police Act, 41 Geo. III (British Museum, Local Acts (1801) c. cxxvi).

Bath Chronicle (Bath Reference Library).

R. Mainwaring: *The Annals of Bath, 1838.*

Appendix of Documents

Appendix A

A CHARTIST POSTER, 1841
TO THE POOR OF BATH!

On Monday next a Public Meeting is to be held at the Guildhall, to consider the best means to relieve your sufferings. Mr. Hunt, the LIBERAL Mayor of the city, will preside. The object of the Meeting is, doubtless, most laudable, if properly carried out. But what do you suppose will be resolved upon to allay your miseries and improve your condition? Will it be endeavoured to remove THE CAUSE of your distress? Will anything be said of the enormous TAXES you have to pay? Or your unjust exclusion from your NATURAL RIGHTS the enjoyment of which would protect you and render you prosperous and happy? NO! It will be agreed to raise a subscription by which a few loaves of bread and baskets of coal may be doled out among you — CHARITY will be extended to a small degree, but JUSTICE WILL BE DENIED. Now you should understand this important fact — If JUSTICE WERE DONE YOU, THERE WOULD BE NO NECESSITY FOR CHARITY. You have to pay the Queen every year £300,000 and much more; Prince Albert, £30,000; Queen Dowager, £100,000; Duchess of Kent, £30,000; King of Hanover, £21,000; AND MANY MILLIONS OF MONEY MORE ARE EVERY YEAR EXTORTED FROM YOU. To pay this, your bread is taxed, your meat is taxed, the tea you drink is taxed, the fire that warms you is taxed, everything you hear, see, feel, smell, or taste is taxed to an enormous extent. IF A POOR MAN EARNS ONE POUND, FIFTEEN SHILLINGS ARE TAKEN FROM HIM IN DIRECT AND INDIRECT TAXES ! ! You will be told this promotes the good of the People — the money 'goes off' in a waterspout and returns in refreshing dews!' But you feel the want of the DEW just now — and those who impoverish you, CHARITABLY give a crust of bread, to keep you from starving. The thief throws the dog a bone to keep it from barking: you are to be quiet when good people are kind and generous!

SUFFERERS — You are oppressed, but have no power to rid yourselves of oppression. The power has been wrested and witheld from you — you have been robbed of your rights, which is THE CAUSE of your

105

destitution . . . It is time, however, THE SYSTEM should be changed, and Honest Popular Government be established, which alone can permanently benefit the Working Classes.

Attend the Meeting in thousands. Come in your rags and tattered garments. Bring your pining infants and sorrowing parents; hear your woes lamented by men who assist to cause them, by aiding to exclude you from political power, which would protect you, and render your honest labour of proper value. But do not disperse until you declare that you are dealt unjustly with. Some of your own class will be there to advocate your cause. Some of your fellow sufferers will assert and defend your rights. Be there at the appointed time — be peaceable, behave respectful — but do not separate when you have met, without proclaiming that you are sensible of the wrongs you endure. The Repeal of no law; the enactment of the Ballot; the passing of no partial measure of Parliament; nor the CHARITY of pretended friends, can PERMANENTLY benefit you. YOU MUST HAVE THE POWER OF ELECTING REPRESENT-ATIVES, WHO SHALL WATCH OVER YOUR INTERESTS, AND PROTECT YOU FROM THAT OPPRESSION WHICH MUST EVER BE THE INEVITABLE RESULT OF THE EXCLUSIVE RE-PRESENTATION OF THE WEALTHY CLASSES.

REMEMBER: THE MEETING IS CALLED FOR MONDAY, at ONE o'CLOCK

(January 9th, 1841).

Appendix B

RULES OF THE TEXTILE FACTORY AT TWERTON, 1832

From the great increase of beer-houses in this parish, and the consequent increased drinking which it has occasion much to the injury both of the workpeople and ourselves, we have considered it absolutely necessary, as much for their benefit and respectability as for our own protection, to enforce the following:

RULES AND REGULATIONS:

1st.   Any person whatsoever who shall leave his or her work without first informing the clerk or foreman of their respective shop of such their intention shall be fined 1s.

2nd.   Any sloober who shall, without permission, leave his employment, by which the work of his engines, and feeders and piecers, must necessarily be suspended, will, in addition to the fine, be required to pay the amount of such feeders and piecers wages.

3rd. Any mule-spinner absenting himself without leave will also be required, in addition to the fine, to pay for the lost time of the piecers.

4th. Any weaver having a loom driven by power absenting himself without leave for part of a day shall be fined 1s., and for a whole day 2s.

5th. Any young woman found drinking in a public-house at any time, whether during the hours of work or not, will be liable to a fine of 1s., and such who may make a practice of frequenting public houses will on no account be employed in any capacity whatever. It is hoped that young women who are disposed to live respectably will consider it a disgrace to associate with such persons.

6th. Incomings, or what are called shop dues, of any kind whatever, are strictly forbidden; and if any such should be enforced, the parties concerned shall be fined in the full amount of the dues paid; but no fine will be considered a sufficient compensation for such a breach of rules. As it is scarcely possible this rule can be evaded without the knowledge of the foreman of the shop, he will be held responsible, and fined in the same amount as the parties so offending.

7th. All waste or sweeping is to be removed daily from each shop to a place appointed, and for any neglect in this respect the shop will be fined 2s. 6d.

8th. Every power-weaver is required to clean the gear, and all other parts of his loom, at least once a week, under a penalty of 1s.

9th. All workmen are required to keep their respective windows clean, and to pay for such as may be broken. In case of necessity, the foreman will decide to whom any window shall belong.

10th. A book will be kept for the entry of all offences, and for an account of imperfect and bad work of all kinds, to which reference will be made from time to time; and such workmen who shall be often found infringing these rules, or otherwise negligent in their work, will be discharged.

11th. All money paid as fines shall go to form a fund for the relief of those who are in sickness or distress, the management of which shall be under the direction of a committee selected from the most respectable of workmen.

(*Report of the Factory Commissioners, 1833*).

Appendix C

THE BATH ELECTION, 1832

THE Nomination of two fit and proper Persons to serve in the Reformed Parliament for the City of Bath took place yesterday (Monday).

The hustings were erected on the Eastern side of the Orange Grove, opposite the Abbey. They were extremely well constructed; and the area in front of them was one of very considerable extent; affording standing room for a much larger number of persons than the Constituency of Bath amount to. This being the first popular election that has taken place in Bath, the Mayor (W. CLARK, esq.) deserves great credit for his judicious arrangements on the occasion. A very convenient situation was set apart for the Gentlemen of the Press; an act of consideration on the part of His Worship which we desire gratefully to acknowledge.

At a little after 10 o'clock Mr. HOBHOUSE (one of the Candidates) appeared. He was received with groans and hisses from the people present, but who at that time did not probably exceed 300. Their number, however, rapidly increased.

Soon afterwards, Mr. ROEBUCK, preceded by a band of music, and surrounded by his Committee, entered the Grove. (The Hon. Candidate had breakfasted with his Vice-President in the Circus, whence he proceeded to his Committee Room, attended by about 400 of his friends, all respectable individuals). By this time, the multitude had greatly increased; and they received the popular Candidate with the most cordial greetings. Several appropriate flags, and banners bearing devices, imparted éclat to Mr. Roebuck's party: the mottoes we noticed were, 'Equal Rights' — 'Britons never more will be slaves' — 'Parliamentary Reform Jubilee, 1832', on a pillar, supported by 'Magna Charta' — 'Bill of Rights' — 'Reform Bill'. Another, 'All we ask is equal rights'. The multitude had now very greatly increased, and numerous electioneering jokes were elicited: such as, 'Take care of the wild beasts'. Then some ingenious biped would imitate the braying of an ass, which excited much laughter. Various other allusions to the usual occupants of a menagerie continued to be made by the people; all of which excited the risibilities of the bystanders. Indeed the people seemed to be very good-tempered, and cheered every jest that was broached respecting the Election; as if determined to be merry . . .

General PALMER came on the hustings the last of the Candidates; he was very well received.

On Mr. HOBHOUSE presenting himself in front of the hustings, not above 50 hats were waved in the air, while the rest of the people, now amounting (at a quarter before eleven) to not less than 5,000, testified their dislike of him by hisses and groans . . .

At the request of Mr. ROEBUCK, Mr. CRISP now addressed the

people through a speaking trumpet, entreating them to give every one a fair hearing. (Cries of 'Roebuck shall get in, whether or no.') . . .

As soon as the Mayor had ascertained that the Abbey clock had struck eleven, he ordered the Town Crier to ring his bell, as the signal for the commencement of the proceedings. The Town Clerk (P. George, Esq.) now read the precept to the Sheriff of Somersetshire. The oath to the Mayor, as the returning officer for the City of Bath, was next administered by the Town Clerk; by whom also the Act against Bribery was read . . .

(*Bath and Cheltenham Gazette, 11th December, 1832*).

Appendix D

BATH'S SLUMS, 1842

. . . The Rev. Whitwell Elwin has supplied the following return of the chances of life amongst the different classes in that city. Out of 616 cases of death in 1840, the results were as follows:

No. of deaths	Average Age of Deceased
146 Gentlemen, professional persons, and their families	55
244 Tradesmen and their families ..	37
896 Mechanics, labourers, and their families	25

The very high average chances of life amongst the middle classes, which is nearly the same as that of the farmers, etc. of the agricultural districts, is the fact adduced as most strongly proving the salubrity of the place . . .

'. . . And herein, it appears to me [says Mr. Elwin], consists the value of the return. It shows that the congregation of men is not of necessity unhealthy; nay, that towns, possessing as they do superior medical skill and readier access to advice, may, under favourable circumstances, have an advantage over the country. The situation of the tradesmen of Bath, inferior as it is to that of the gentry, is better than that of their own station in other places. The streets they chiefly inhabit, though with many exceptions, are wide, and swept by free currents of air, with houses large and well ventilated. The condition of the poor is worse than would be anticipated from the other portions of the town. They are chiefly located in low districts at the bottom of the valley, and narrow alleys and confined courts are very numerous . . .

... Whatever influence occupation and other circumstances may have upon mortality, no one can inspect the registers without being struck by the deteriorated value of life in inferior localities, even where the inhabitants were the same in condition with those who lived longer in better situations ...

... The deaths from fever and contagious diseases I found to be almost exclusively confined to the worst parts of the town. An epidemic of smallpox raged at the end of the year 1837, and carried off upwards of 300 persons; yet of all this number I do not think there was a single gentleman, and not above two or three tradesmen. The residences of the labouring classes were pretty equally visited, disease showing here and there a predilection for particular spots, and settling with full virulence in Avon-street and its offsets. I went through the registers from the commencement, and observed that, whatever contagious or epidemic diseases prevailed—fever, smallpox, influenza—this was the scene of its principal ravages; and its is the very place of which every person acquainted with Bath would have predicted this result. Everything vile and offensive is congregated there. All the scum of Bath—its low prostitutes, its thieves, its beggars—are piled up in the dens rather than houses of which the street consists. Its population is the most disproportioned to the accommodation of any I have ever heard; and to aggravate the mischief, the refuse is commonly thrown under the staircase; and water more scarce than in any quarter of the town. It would hardly be an hyperbole to say that there is less water consumed than beer; and altogether it would be more difficult to exaggerate the description of this dreadful spot than to convey an adequate notion to those who have never seen it. A prominent feature in the midst of this mass of physical and moral evils is the extraordinary number of illegitimate children; the off-spring of persons who in all respects live together as man and wife. Without the slightest objection to the legal obligation, the moral degradation is such that marriage is accounted a superfluous ceremony, not worth the payment of the necessary fees; and on one occasion, when it was given out that these would be dispensed with, upwards of 50 persons from Avon-street, who had lived together for years, voluntarily came forward to enter into a union. And thus it invariably happens in crowded haunts of sin and filth, where principle is obliterated, and where public opinion, which so often operates in the place of principle, is never heard; where, to say truth, virtue is treated with the scorn which in better society is accorded to vice ...'

(*Report of Sanitary Commissioners, 1842;* p.p., Lords (1842), Vol. XXVI).

Appendix E

A DRAMATIC FETE, 1831

... The novel species of amusement to which we allude, is that now well established, and extensively patronized annual Dramatic Fête, the first of which was held at the Bath Theatre, on the 23rd April, 1824. Each succeeding season, this splendid fête has been repeated; and, as it forms by far the most prominent feature in the sound of attractions which a Bath season presents, we will now endeavour to describe it.

The Theatre, on this occasion, is entirely devoted to the species of entertainment which the name bespeaks, the whole area being laid out as a magnificent saloon. Suspended immediately over the proscenium, is a chandelier of bronzed metal, twelve feet high and six in diameter, and containing three hundred fleur-de-lys jet lights, which diffuse a rich, though soft brilliancy, to the most remote corners of the building. On entering the Theatre, the ante-room is discovered, fitted up as a splendid marqueê; its floor being covered with crimson cloth, which extends the whole length of the lobbies and stair cases; and the entire area of the pit is covered by a platform, on a level with, and forming a continuation of the proscenium. The saloon above is set apart for refreshments, and the gallery for spectators only. The subordinate decorations of the interior are extremely elegant, varying each year, according to the taste of those who kindly undertake the management and superintendence.

The company begin to assemble at nine; and, in the space of half an hour, the Theatre becomes filled to the very roof. A humorous dramatic piece then commences (generally of one act), which is performed sometimes by professional gentlemen; and at others by amateurs. After this the curtain rises, and ranges of tables are discovered, extending down the sides and across the centre, loaded with delicacies of every description—After the national anthem, by the entire vocal strength of the Theatre, the company leave their boxes, and the area, extending in length nearly one hundred and twenty feet, soon becomes filled, the whole of which presents to the eye one rich and gorgeous scene. All shades and tints, from the glowing hues of oriental costume, 'to spotless white and solemn black'— rich military and naval uniforms, and every costume that fancy or caprice can invent, are here displayed. The remainder of the night is passed in the giddy mazes of the dance; and the national anthem, by the orchestra, closes the exhilarating scene.

It has been repeatedly asserted, by those competent to judge, that this splendid fête is not surpassed, in magnificence and brilliancy of effect, by any of those witnessed either in London or the Continental capitals.

We have been thus minuted in the description of the chief characteristics of this splendid annual fête, because, as a public entertainment, it interests a large portion of the trading community and inhabitants of the city; and

111

from its peculiar attractions, and over-flowing support, ranks highest among the amusements of the season.

(R. Mainwaring: *Annals of Bath, 1838*).

Appendix F

THE OPENING OF THE G.W.R., 1841

The entire line, as had been announced, was opened to the public on 30th June and now trains are running regularly, according to the hours stated, between those places, and, still further, on the Bristol and Exeter lines as far as Bridgwater. The last and greatest difficulty of this superb railway—the Boxhill Tunnel—is now triumphantly overcome, and, independent of the utility to agriculture, to manufactures, to commerce, and to intelligence of this free and rapid communication between the great ports of London and Bristol, it remains a splendid monument of the industry and of the genius of this country, equal, if not superior, to any that the ingenuity and perseverance of man have ever accomplished. Early on Wednesday morning, the first train from Chippenham to Bath— that part of the line which hitherto was unopened—started under the conduct of Mr. Brunel, who found everything in complete order, and expressed himself perfectly satisfied with his expeditionary trip. After the first essay of the road had been made, and when the friends of the undertaking who could absent themselves for the day from the polling booths had mustered, Mr. George Burge, of Herne Bay, the contractor, together with Messrs. Brewer and Lewis, and a large party, accompanied by a band of music, with flags and banners proceeded through the tunnel, which was lighted throughout, and which really presented a most extra-ordinary appearance. While making this procession, three trains, crowded with people passed through, and nothing could exceed their astonishment at seeing a splendid procession 300 feet underground, literally 'within the bowels of the earth', and at hearing the strange music, which, from the echo by which the band was attended, produced a most singular effect. The examination of this stupendous tunnel being completed, and the exploring party having returned, refreshments were served in a handsome tent, which had been erected for that purpose, between the imposing grand arch of the tunnel and the beautiful Corsham-road Bridge, which (being technically called a jack-arch) is a very model of architecture. In order that our readers may form some idea of the Boxhill Tunnel, we may here remark that it is within a few yards of two miles in length, that it runs 306 below the surface of the earth, and that a great portion of it has been

112

Appendices

cut out of the solid rock. One mile and a quarter of this is lined with masonry; the quantity of excavation was about 300,000 yards, and the number of bricks used was near twenty millions. One ton of gunpowder was used for blasting and one ton of candles were consumed per week for upwards of two years and a half, and 300 horses have been daily employed in it. The solidity of the work, the symmetry of the entire arch, and the beauty of its two fronts, built of picked Bath stone, commended universal admiration; and too much praise cannot be given to the contractors, Mr. Burge, and Messrs. Brewer and Lewis, for the finished and workmanlike manner in which they had performed their contracts. The three great *desiderata* of a tunnel, viz: absence from danger, darkness and damp, have been in this perfectly acquired. It is so dry that one might walk through it in slippers. It is lighted by six shafts, which give by day a very sufficient light, and is as safe as any part of the line. The resident engineer, Mr. Wm. Glennie, and his assistants, were highly and deservedly complimented by the directors present for their assiduity and skill; and the unwearied attention of Mr. Brunel received their warmest approbation and thanks. In the evening, the contractors, directors, and gentlemen present, dined together and forgot their disappointment of the grand entertainment expected on Monday, in a merry, though small party, when the prosperity of the company, and the healths of all concerned in forwarding its interests, were drunk in 'potations pottle deep' of sparkling champagne and brimming cups of purple claret. Not the slightest accident occurred during the day, and everything connected with the opening of the Great Western Railway passed off most satisfactorily.

(Bath Chronicle, August 1841).

Appendix G

BATH TURNPIKE TRUSTS

NOTICE is hereby given, that the TOLLS arising at the several Toll Gates or Bars hereafter mentioned, will be LET by AUCTION to the best Bidder, at the GUILDHALL in Bath, on THURSDAY, the 12th day of March next, between the hours of Twelve at noon and Two in the afternoon, in One or Two Lots, as may be then determined on, for the term of Three Years, to commence from the 14th day of May next, in the manner directed by the Acts passed in the 3rd and 4th Years of the reign of his late Majesty King George the 4th, 'for regulating Turnpike Roads;' which Tolls produced the last year the undermentioned Sums above the expences of collecting them, and will be put up at such Sums, or in one Sum, as the

113

Trustees shall think fit, under and subject to such conditions as shall be then produced.

Whoever happens to be the best bidder, must at the same time pay one month in advance, if required, of the rent at which such Tolls may be left, and give security, with sufficient sureties to the satisfaction of the said Trustees, for payment of such rent monthly, or in such other proportions as shall be directed—Dated 9th February, 1835.

	£
1st Lot. The London, Batheaston, Lansdown, Holloway, Greenaway Lane, Burnthouse, Combe Down, Combe Hill, Red Post, Cross Post, Lower Bristol, Kelston, Weston, Marksbury, and White Cross Gates and Bars	10,360
2nd Lot. The Box Gate on the New Road	555

P. George, *Clerk to the said Trustees.*

(*Bath Chronicle*, 10th February, 1835).

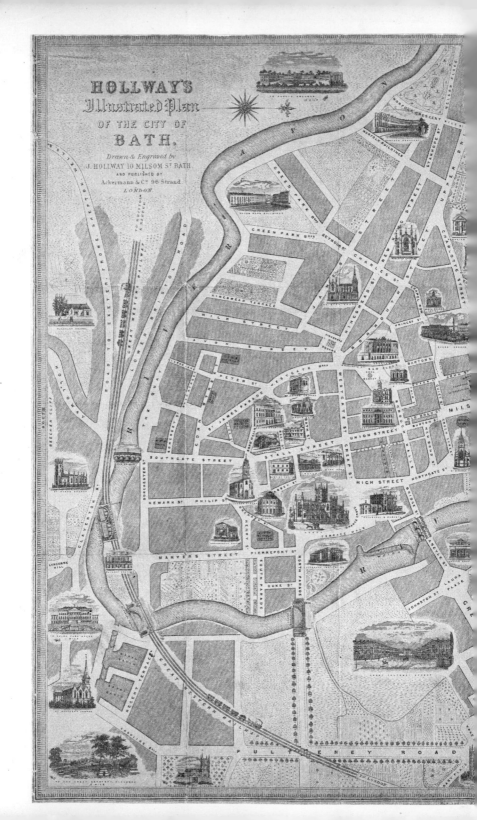